The Black
Academic's Guide
to Winning Tenure—
Without Losing
Your Soul

The Black
Academic's Guide
to Winning Tenure—
Without Losing
Your Soul

Kerry Ann Rockquemore
Tracey Laszloffy

LYNNE
RIENNER
PUBLISHERS

BOULDER
LONDON

Published in the United States of America in 2008 by
Lynne Rienner Publishers, Inc.
1800 30th Street, Boulder, Colorado 80301
www.rienner.com

and in the United Kingdom by
Lynne Rienner Publishers, Inc.
Gray's Inn House, 127 Clerkenwell Road, London EC1 5DB

Library of Congress Cataloging-in-Publication Data
Rockquemore, Kerry.
   The black academic's guide to winning tenure—without losing your soul /
Kerry Ann Rockquemore, Tracey Laszloffy.
      p. cm.
   Includes index.
   ISBN 978-1-58826-562-3 (hardcover : alk. paper)
   ISBN 978-1-58826-588-3 (pbk. : alk. paper)
   1. College teachers—Tenure—United States. 2. African American college teachers.
I. Laszloffy, Tracey A.   II. Title.
   LB2335.7.R63 2008
   378.1'21408996073—dc22

                                                      2008006784

British Cataloguing in Publication Data
A Cataloguing in Publication record for this book
is available from the British Library.

Printed and bound in the United States of America

∞   The paper used in this publication meets the requirements
    of the American National Standard for Permanence of
    Paper for Printed Library Materials Z39.48-1992.

15

Contents

Acknowledgments

THE BLACK ACADEMIC'S GUIDE to *Winning Tenure—Without Losing Your Soul* has traveled a long and winding road to publication, and we want to warmly thank all those who participated in its creation and development. The first thing on Kerry Ann's list of "Things to Do Once I Win Tenure" was "start a mentoring program for black faculty that actually works." Because she had been so poorly counseled, she wanted to start a radically different program for faculty of color—one that would help individuals to make the transition from graduate student to professor. She was certain that nobody should have to walk a path full of pitfalls alone, learn by trial and error, or fail because of a lack of information. Her ideas for an Under-Represented Faculty Mentoring Program were warmly supported by her colleagues at the University of Illinois at Chicago (UIC): Beth Richie, Tyrone Forman, Amanda Lewis, Javette Orgain, Curtisteen Steward, Michael Toney, Danny Martin, and W. Clarke Douglas. The program never would have moved forward had it not been for the first group of enthusiastic junior faculty: Michelle Boyd, Cynthia Blair, and David Stovall. Out of that small endeavor, a campus-wide initiative developed from the bottom up and flourished with the financial support of the Chancellor's Committee on the Status of Blacks and the Provost's Office at UIC.

The black junior faculty who participated in the Under-Represented Faculty Mentoring Program were generous, honest, and very clear that they wanted information in a central location. They did not want to be wholly dependent on one mentoring "guru" who would dispense knowledge at the whim of that person's schedule or inclination. More than anything, they wanted to know how to be successful despite any racism they might experience in their departments—and how to achieve that success with their heads held high, integrity intact, and as true black intellectuals. We want to thank those who participated in the mentoring program, including Connie Dallas, Benet Deberry-Spence, Sabine French, Kim Gomez, Mark Grevious, Emily Guss, Marisha Humphries, Yolanda Majors, Alicia Matthews, Cassandra McKay, Steve Simms, Chedgzsey McKeever, Chyvette Williams, Ivy Wilson, Bernadette Pruitt, Eddy Kornegay, Jemima Pierre, Badia Ahad, Rosamond King, and Carmen Lilly. Their enthusiastic participation, clarity about their needs, and honest feedback were invaluable. Kuliva Wilburn and Erin Starkey held it all together organizationally by drawing on their superior report writing, evaluation, and community-organizing skills. Senior faculty members Tyrone Forman, Phil Bowman, Barbara Ransby, Charles Mills, Cedric Herring, Sharon Collins, Sharon Holland, and Beth Richie all shared concrete advice during our mentoring panels. Their strategies and tips underlie the core information in *The Black Academic's Guide to Winning Tenure—Without Losing Your Soul*, and we hope that through its publication, their generosity of spirit, time, and energy will be an ongoing gift to others.

All good things must come to an end, as did our mentoring program. While our goal was institutionalization, achieving that goal swept in new leadership, programming, and support and swept out the faculty-driven spirit of collaboration, community building, and collective mentoring that made the program successful. Freshly dethroned, Kerry Ann finally had time to commit to paper all of the wisdom that was conveyed through the mentoring panels. To partner in this task, she turned to the one person who had helped her to successfully navigate the treacherous terrain of her own tenure-track journey: Tracey Laszloffy. Tracey's experience working with black professionals in the context of therapy and as a popular faculty coach enabled an analysis of the deeper systemic and psychological pressures facing black faculty as they move toward tenure and promotion.

We were fortunate to have an encouraging and enthusiastic editor in Leanne Anderson at Lynne Rienner Publishers, who has nurtured this project through to completion even when we felt like giving up. Our first draft was read by several attentive and engaged readers, including Rainier Spencer, Eileen McConnell, Binta Alleyne, Cassandra McKay, Anna Branch, and LaShawn Stinson; thank you all. We also thank LRP's anonymous reviewers. And while there are too many to name, we are deeply grateful to the many black faculty who participated in the workshops where we tested, refined, and organized the material that became this book. Your openness, honesty, and willingness to share your experiences with us in the context of the workshops have helped us to both sharpen and soften the material where needed.

Beyond our gratitude to all of those who directly supported our writing activity, we wish to thank those who encouraged us intellectually and personally throughout the process. Kerry Ann has been blessed by the support of the African American Studies Department at UIC under the leadership of Beth Richie and Paul Zeleza. Special thanks go to the members of the BlackAcademic.com daily writing forum, who keep us accountable for our writing on a *daily* basis, and whose willingness to share their questions, concerns, ideas, and experiences has greatly enriched the content and flavor of this book.

Finally, we are both deeply supported by loving families, friends, and partners without whom we would not have completed this project. Kerry Ann thanks her husband, William, who has supported her unconditionally and in every way imaginable throughout her academic career. Tracey thanks both her partner, Bill, for his unwavering encouragement and support, and her family, especially her parents, June and Jerry, whose faith in her capabilities and unconditional positive regard are the greatest gifts possible.

In addition to all of this considerable support, *The Black Academic's Guide to Winning Tenure—Without Losing Your Soul* was most profoundly shaped by the black faculty who have shared their triumphs and, more importantly, their pain with us. During interviews, in therapy, at conferences, in their homes, and at chance meetings, we have never been short of people willing to share their stories with us in the spirit of both getting this book to print and helping others to have a clearer path toward the twin goals of tenure and the proliferation of black professors in the academy.

1 How to Win Tenure— Without Losing Your Soul

COLLEGE and university officials regularly bemoan the lack of diversity among their faculty and the challenges in recruiting and retaining faculty of color. They have good reason for concern because an examination of the statistics on faculty diversity in higher education reveals a dismal state of affairs that has changed little since the passage of civil rights legislation. In fact, less than 5 percent of faculty at all US colleges and universities are black, and the largest percentage of black scholars is employed at historically black colleges and universities. Based on the lack of progress in diversifying the faculties at predominately white institutions, most observers agree that past diversity efforts have been insufficient and have largely failed to produce the desired outcome: a faculty that reflects the diverse racial and ethnic composition of our nation.

There are complex reasons why bright and motivated black students do not end up on the faculties of US colleges and universities. Scholarly attention has focused at various points of the academic pipeline, including the quality of public schooling; access to undergraduate education; the effects of "weeding courses" in the first year of the undergraduate experience; the lack of mentoring and role models; difficult transitions to graduate school; differential treatment during the graduate school experience; the lure of alternative market sectors; the structure of the academic job market; and institutional recruitment, promotion, and retention policies. Clearly, the unchanging statistics reflect structural problems in our educational system that span from primary schools to universities. Although there are numerous possible points of intervention for each of these structural problems, this book is directed toward individual faculty members seeking to succeed in institutions that are not designed for their

1

success. While it is abundantly clear that structural solutions are needed for structural problems in US higher education, it is equally clear that abstract discussions of structural problems and policy solutions are rarely helpful to first-year faculty trying to make the transition from graduate student to professor. In other words, there has been precious little attention devoted to the daily struggles of individual black faculty and the concrete steps that they can take to succeed in spite of the forces that are pushing against them.

Life on the tenure track is a difficult experience for all junior faculty, irrespective of race, ethnicity, gender, sexual orientation, class, or nationality. Six years of probation can feel like an eternity when faced with unclear and ever-rising expectations, lack of support, subjective evaluations, and limited external validation. All junior faculty members are in a vulnerable position because their institutional rank and position grant them less power in relation to senior colleagues who vote on their tenure. Because interactions between senior and junior faculty are defined by unequal power, all challenges, disagreements, and conflicts must be handled in calculated ways that reflect the utmost diplomacy.

While *institutional hierarchies* leave all junior faculty in a vulnerable position, the difficulty associated with the probationary period is intensified for faculty who occupy a disadvantaged position within one or more of the *social hierarchies* structured around race, class, gender, sexual orientation, and nationality. For white male faculty, the one-down position associated with being a junior faculty member is a temporary status that is confined to the institutional hierarchy. For black faculty, their job-related one-down status does not end at the walls of the institution. Whatever insensitivities and indignities they suffer on campus because of their social location exist beyond the campus, and will continue to exist if or when they are promoted with tenure. So, we take as our most basic premise that there is a fundamental difference between the experiences of black and white faculty, and that difference is caused by the fact that we live in a social world organized by race. All faculty experience vulnerability, but that vulnerability is role specific and finite for some, while for others it exists within a broader context of societal racial inequalities.

The racial hierarchy in the United States not only dictates that black faculty are in a permanent one-down status across social contexts, but also infiltrates academic institutions, influencing how black and white faculty experience the very same departments. Who receives the benefit of the doubt, whose opinion is valued, who gets mentored, and who is invited into collaborative opportunities are subtly shaped by often unconscious racialized assumptions about who is an insider and who is an outsider, who does and does not belong in the academic club, and whose presence is welcomed and whose is tolerated. As a result, the reality of life on the tenure track for many black academics is one in which they struggle with racial subjugation both inside and outside of their respective campus.

Having survived graduate school and the academic job market, many new PhDs enter their first job with high expectations. They often imagine the colleges and universities that employ them will be bastions of progressive liberalism that will challenge the evils of classism, racism, sexism, and homophobia and practice equity and social justice. After all, most colleges' mission statements articulate a commitment to the production of knowledge, the transformation of the social world, and service in the pursuit of justice. Even having faced discriminatory treatment in graduate school, many black academics imagine that their experience will be fundamentally different because of their new and upwardly mobile status as professor, even if it is assistant professor.

By the time black faculty reach the end of their first year, many have become painfully aware that they have not escaped the indignities and frustrations with respect to racism and discrimination that they experienced as graduate students. In fact, many begrudgingly realize that, because they are one of few black faculty on campus, they face disproportionately higher service requests than their colleagues, are overwhelmed by black students seeking a role model, and are expected to "prove" themselves in ways that their white colleagues are not. Those who were naïve in the negotiation process also realize that they are being paid less, are teaching more, and are receiving fewer resources than their better-informed and better-mentored white colleagues. Very quickly, many new black faculty realize the hard facts about being black on the tenure track: that they face the same demands as their white counterparts *and* they also must negotiate both nuanced racial insensitivities and outright racial insults.

This painful realization is often followed by a typical trajectory in which a young black faculty member who was barely mentored in graduate school takes several years on the job to figure out (through trial and error) what it means to be a professor. While all new faculty struggle in the transition from graduate student to professor, faculty of color must learn how to simultaneously juggle the excessive and never-ending service demands that result from being the only black faculty member (or one of a few) in their department, college, or university in addition to the alienation and hostility they may experience on campus.

As junior faculty, we both faced the dilemma of realizing that the institutions in which we were embedded were not set up for us to succeed and, yet, we had to succeed anyway. By virtue of our different racial locations (Kerry Ann is black and Tracey is white), we directly observed, experienced, and commiserated about the similar experiences we had as female faculty and the different experiences we had based on our race. While we made different decisions and our careers took different twists and turns along the way, we are clear today that no black faculty member should have to start from scratch, or go through the misery of learning from costly mistakes, humiliating incidents, or hindsight after getting passed over.

Although neither of us ever imagined writing a book on mentoring, we wrote this book because we see the same pattern of mistakes, conflicts, and tensions played out repeatedly in the lives of black faculty. Whether it is among faculty in Kerry Ann's mentoring program, Tracey's clients in private practice, or the hundreds of faculty we have met in the process of presenting our workshops, it is the same story over and over and over again: black faculty, by and large, are not being mentored and are experiencing institutional alienation, isolation, and hostility. Too much time and emotional energy are being wasted by individual faculty trying to figure out the basic elements of what it means to be a successful new professor: how to teach well and efficiently, how to manage time spent on service, and how to publish prolifically. Because black faculty must do this even as they negotiate subtle and overt racial slights and assaults, it can be a particularly difficult transition. In short, we want to help every reader develop the strategies and techniques that are necessary to win tenure, while acknowledging that this is especially challenging for black faculty. Our purpose in this book is to pass on to black academics those strategies and techniques that have worked for many black faculty who have succeeded in winning tenure.

While we are concerned with helping faculty to become productive and efficient, and to meet their institutional criteria for promotion (i.e., how to win tenure), we are even more deeply concerned about how to do so without losing your soul. We know far too many black faculty who have sacrificed everything—their relationships, their voice, their integrity—in the process of pursuing tenure and promotion. Inevitably, they win tenure, but have become so alienated from their self in the process that they can no longer connect to who they are and where they are going. They have so deeply internalized the expectations, attitudes, and judgments of those around them that they are unable to evaluate their own self-worth beyond their next grant, publication, or award. In other words, they played the game to win so intensely that they sacrificed their core self in the process and internalized their institution's values as their own criteria for determining self-worth. Regrettably, we know many more black faculty who lost their soul in the process, and *still* did not win tenure. These are the most unfortunate cases because they require both a personal and professional resurrection.

Toward our secondary goal of learning to navigate the minefield of the tenure process without losing your voice and integrity, we spend considerable time clarifying how black faculty can better understand the system in which they are embedded, recognize the racialized dynamics of that system, understand what they bring to the equation, and learn how to locate their own sources of power to navigate their way to promotion with integrity. Spending six years in an institutionally vulnerable position does not mean that you are powerless as an individual. By understanding who you are and where you are located, you can avoid being passively controlled and devalued in your environment by developing a mental framework of independence, a personal definition of success, a clear plan for achieving it, and real support systems to lean on in difficult times. More concretely, we believe the best way for you to win tenure without losing your soul is to (1) learn the rules of the game, (2) master your technique, and (3) play to win on both the personal and professional levels.

Centering the Black Academic Experience

As the title of this book makes evident, our target audience is black academics who are on the road to tenure. On many occasions, we have been challenged about what makes the recommendations that we present in this book exclusive to black faculty. To clarify, most of the nuts-and-bolts suggestions we provide for how to win tenure are not exclusive to black faculty and can be used by faculty of any race. However, despite the fact that black and white faculty are the same in terms of their capabilities, their tenure journeys are made distinct by the intervening effects of racism. Throughout the book, we have taken great pains to contextualize generic concepts and strategies to take into account how racism shapes the experiences of black junior faculty.

On a similar note, we also have been challenged at times about why we elected to focus so narrowly on racism as an intervening factor while excluding consideration of other forms of oppression that share much in common with racism. We agree that the dynamics of racism and other manifestations of oppression share similarities. Therefore, although we specifically focus on racism and black academics, we acknowledge that much of the material we present can be applied to understanding and addressing how other forms of oppression shape the tenure process for members of oppressed groups who are underrepresented in higher education.

We wrote this book with black faculty in mind, but we recognize that other racial minorities also face racism and struggle with similar racial issues and dilemmas faced by black academics. Initially, we considered defining our target audience as *people of color*, but rejected this term because it fails to recognize the objective and subjective differences that exist between groups as well as the group-specific assumptions, negative stereotypes, and biases associated with blackness. Readers from other racial minority groups may find some issues we explore to be consistent with their own experience at the same time that others do not apply. Regrettably, the vast majority of professional development resources for new faculty are either silent on the issue of race or contain a single chapter to address *all* underrepresented groups and their concerns. This seems insufficient, centers on white male academics, and reinforces the notion that the concerns of everyone else are the same and can be summarized and addressed in a brief separate chapter. Ultimately, we wrote this book for black faculty as a way of moving the group from the margins to the center of discourse on professional development and faculty retention.

Organization of the Book

Our point of departure for winning tenure without losing your soul is an articulation of the "rules of the game." We do this by providing an overview of how the realities of race manifest in academic contexts by identifying the specific ways that race and power converge to shape life in the academy for black faculty in "Race, Power, and the Academic System" (Chapter 2). Thus, for most black readers, Part 1, "Understanding the Game," merely serves to make explicit that which is intuitively and experientially understood on a daily basis. In "The Politics of 'Fit'" (Chapter 3), we explore the importance of "goodness-of-fit" between your personal system orientation and the dynamics of the academic system in which you are embedded. In addition to helping you identify your personal orientation and your system's orientation, we discuss what you can do in situations where there is a poor fit.

Part 2, "Mastering Your Technique," identifies the core set of skills and techniques that all junior faculty need to successfully make the transition from graduate student to professor. It is crucial for black faculty to master these skills and techniques because each mistake will be highly visible and any perceived lack of productivity is unlikely to be overlooked. This section begins with "Tenure and Time Management" (Chapter 4) and "The Academic Office" (Chapter 5), which address three core skills that form a necessary foundation for success: strategic planning, time management, and the development of an organizational system that works for you. The remaining two chapters in this section, "Healthy Pathways to Publication" (Chapter 6) and "The Art of Efficient Teaching and Service" (Chapter 7), provide in-depth considerations of the three factors that are most critical for tenure and promotion: publication, teaching, and service. We focus on how to develop a consistent writing routine and proactively create accountability mechanisms; how to teach efficiently; and how to participate in a reasonable amount of service to the department, college, and the university community without falling into the trap of service overload. Although the weight put on each of these components varies by the type and culture of institution you work in (community college, liberal arts college, or university), it is imperative to demonstrate competence in each of these areas early on and to move toward excellence over your probationary period.

Having established how race and power interact to shape the dynamics in your institution, how to assess and enhance the compatibility between your system orientation and your system, and how to master the core areas in which you will be evaluated, Part 3 is devoted to "Playing to Win." This section focuses on the most critical and challenging component of life on the tenure track: your integrity and your relationships. Winning tenure without losing your soul requires self-awareness, self-knowledge, and self-mastery. The first aspect of your self that we focus on is your response to oppression. In "Shifting from Habits of Survival to Strategies for Success" (Chapter 8), we discuss how individuals develop habitual ways of responding to situations and people who devalue us over the life course. These behavioral responses are grounded in unconscious mental frameworks and are accompanied by emotional reactions. We describe these as "habits of survival" and encourage you to identify your own automatic ways of being and to consider how your habits help and hinder you. This chapter culminates in a consideration of how to shift from habits of survival to strategies for success by making conscious choices about how to respond in different circumstances.

Because conflict is inevitable in all workplaces, but manifests in unique (and often horrifying) ways in the academic workplace, our chapter "Constructive Conflicts" (Chapter 9) addresses how you can engage in healthy conflict with people who have more power than you. Part 3 closes with "Building a Supportive Network" (Chapter 10). Here, we emphasize the importance of proactively establishing and nurturing relationships with people who can provide support and assistance as you begin to build a tenure case that is beyond reproach from the outset of your career.

Cornel West describes being an African American academic as a life of self-imposed marginality. To be black and become an academic requires, to some extent, a disconnection from the wider African American community while, at the same time, never fully being welcomed into the community of the professoriat. The pain, anger, and alienation that are connected to this marginality extract a high price on the physical, mental, and spiritual well-being of black faculty. Though this book will not lay out systematic policy solutions to the persistent problem of faculty diversity, we do hope it helps you, as an individual black faculty member on the front lines, to win tenure without losing your soul in the process.

PART 1
Understanding the Game

2 | Race, Power, and the Academic System

LIKE most organizations, college and university systems are hierarchical and, as a result, power is unequally distributed throughout. In the role of a junior faculty member at your institution, you have power over students and some staff members. However, in relationship to senior colleagues in your department, your lengthy probationary status puts you in a one-down position for six years. Your primary task on the tenure track is to find a way to navigate the system in order to publish your research, teach well, and serve your institution as a good departmental citizen. When you are promoted and awarded tenure, your position and power in the institutional hierarchy will shift dramatically.

Tenure was established to support the concept of academic freedom, which ensures that faculty members have the latitude to explore and express ideas (as radical or unpopular as they may be) without fear of losing their job. Once a junior faculty member receives tenure, he or she has officially arrived into an elite space of privilege. In today's labor market, it is an incredibly rare privilege to possess a professional status that allows the autonomy to pursue your intellectual interests and the security to express ideas that others may find offensive, objectionable, or unpatriotic. The entire purpose of this book is to help you navigate a successful journey into the tenured ranks and to do so with your integrity and voice fully intact. But before we discuss the nuts and bolts of how you can be highly effective in your research, teaching, and service, we need to start by discussing how race and power interact to uniquely shape and complicate the road to tenure for you as a black professor.

Our discussion is not intended to empirically document and persuade majority faculty about the existence of racism in higher education. There are numerous studies that have mapped this terrain (see the

11

recommended reading at the end of this chapter if you want to explore this area further). Instead, we want to sensitize you, as a new faculty member, to the most common ways that black faculty have described their experiences of racism in the academy. This is critically important for three reasons. First and foremost, the nature of racism is to make you (as an individual) think that what you are experiencing is happening *only* to you and that it is an individual (as opposed to systemic) problem. Second, we live in a historical moment and political climate in which the mere mention of race (much less racism) is met with bitter opposition, so you are unlikely to be able to discuss racial experiences openly and honestly with your colleagues without being accused of being "overly sensitive," "playing the race card," or having your concerns dismissed outright. Finally, too many black faculty (particularly those who are not trained in the social and behavioral sciences) find their lack of understanding about the nuanced and covert dynamics of racism in the post–civil rights United States hinders their progress toward tenure and promotion. By the time many have figured out the "race rules" of their institution, it is too late in their trajectory to make the necessary adjustments that may have helped them to individually overcome racial barriers. Our hope is for you to enter your first job with your eyes wide open, attentive to the ways your experience may be different from that of your white colleagues, and with the tools to be successful in spite of the obstacles.

Let us be clear at the outset: life on the tenure track will be one of the most difficult and demanding stages of your academic career because of the high performance expectations, minimal direct feedback, and explicit time constraints of your tenure clock. In this way, all junior faculty members are in a vulnerable one-down position. By definition, as a tenure-track faculty member, you will face an occupational vulnerability that is temporarily restricted to the probationary years, and role specific in terms of consequences. Under normal circumstances, all junior faculty members have their institutional fate discussed, debated, and voted on at multiple institutional levels during the sixth year of their employment. Each junior faculty member will either be denied tenure, which severs the long-term relationship between him or her and the college, or will be awarded tenure, promoted to the rank of associate professor, and ascend to the next level on the college or university's organizational power structure.

In contrast to organizational hierarchies, social hierarchies are not role specific and remain fixed over time. In the United States, social hierarchies exist in relation to various statuses, including race, ethnicity, gender, and sexual orientation, to name but a few. The locations we occupy within each of these social hierarchies shape our social power and privilege accordingly. Because our identities are comprised of multiple dimensions of diversity, we are simultaneously embedded within multiple social hierarchies, some of which grant us considerable power while others grant far less. For example, in terms of race and gender, white female faculty experience a great deal of social power on the basis of race even as they encounter subjugation on the basis of gender (intensely so in the fields where they are grossly underrepresented).

Within colleges and universities, all junior faculty experience a degree of powerlessness as a function of their rank within their institutional hierarchy. But for white junior faculty, this experience is simultaneously time limited and role specific. On the basis of race, they benefit from systematic racial power and privilege within their institutions and society overall. In contrast, black junior faculty encounter the temporary and role-specific vulnerability associated with their institutional rank, as well as systematic racial subjugation, both within their institutions and in society at large. Even after black academics are promoted to tenure and transcend the temporary vulnerability of being untenured, they never transcend their social location based on race. At the end of the day, it is no easier for a tenured versus an untenured black male faculty member to hail a cab. It is the pervasive and non-role specific vulnerability associated with blackness that constitutes the key distinction between the experiences of black and white junior faculty.

Race and power converge to shape every aspect of life within academic institutions. In this section of the book, we identify and explore the most common ways that black faculty describe how their life on the tenure track differs from that of their white counterparts: (1) isolation, alienation, and excessive visibility; (2) classroom hostility; (3) racially based double standards; (4) persistent stereotypes; (5) exclusion from networks; (6) the curse of color blindness; and (7) devaluation and marginalization of scholarship. We describe each of these areas for the purpose of making visible the invisible racialized structures at work in colleges and universities in the United States so that you will be able to recognize and respond to such forces in your institutional environment. All too often, black faculty feel that they are the only ones who see and experience their institution from this perspective and that the racial insults they experience are individual acts of hostility. However, the factors that we outline below represent patterned manifestations of racism throughout the academic system and it is rare to gather a group of black academics where such experiences are not widely experienced.

Isolation, Alienation, and Visibility

With the notable exception of historically black colleges and universities, black faculty are consistently underrepresented in US institutions of higher education. In your institution, there are likely many "zero departments" (those with no black professors whatsoever) and many more where there is only one black faculty member. This is important to observe because, when there are precious few black colleagues in your college or university, a variety of negative consequences can make your first faculty appointment feel like you have joined a "society of one" requiring the payment of the "race tax," special attention to issues of representation, and the careful negotiation of diplomatic relations.

The Race Tax

Having few black faculty members at an institution results in various problems associated with scarcity. Specifically, you may be expected to assume the bulk of service-related demands that involve race or diversity issues. Black faculty are consistently asked to serve on departmental committees that require diverse representation (i.e., a person of color on the committee) as well as on college- and university-level committees that address matters of diversity and equity (i.e., the Provost's Diversity Advisory Committee). Consequently, as a black faculty member, you not only may experience loneliness and isolation because of your solo status, but the fact of your underrepresentation on your institution's faculty will cause you to receive a disproportionately high number of requests for committee- and individual-level service.

Peter was a new assistant professor in the College of Dentistry at a small branch campus of a state university system. In his first semester, he was assigned eight students to supervise during their practicum experience and, of these, four were black, two Latina, and two white. Of the two white students, one was blind and the other was the only openly gay student in the program. Peter asked his department chair why he had assigned him to be solely responsible for "the diversity advising" in the college. In response, the chair explained:

> I realize how this looks, Peter, but you need to understand, we are a small school in a rural community and we only have four faculty of color in the whole university—period! Qualified minorities don't want to come here, which is why we feel privileged that you agreed to come. I know you could have picked a much more prestigious institution. I'm committed to improving how we do diversity, which is

part of why I fought so hard to get you here. The salary we offered you is unprecedented for us, but I know you are worth it, and part of my job is to be sure I use you wisely. The fact is you understand the diversity issues better than most faculty here so it only makes sense to take advantage of that, even though I know it feels unfair to you.

While Peter's department chair was well intentioned, he articulated a common but flawed assumption: that "diversity work" is the responsibility of faculty of color because they are uniquely able to mentor and supervise students of color (and, by extension, white students with some marginalized status). The chair's position supported and enabled the pervasive lack of understanding about diversity among the College of Dentistry's faculty. As long as the chair failed to hold the faculty at large accountable for their inability to effectively mentor and supervise all students in the program, the department would never be transformed. In addition to his advising assignments, Peter had been asked to serve on the college's Diversity Planning Committee and be the "diversity" on three additional committees. Like many black faculty facing the same service pressures, he was at risk of quickly becoming burned out and resentful, yet because of the sheer volume of requests and his uncertainty about the consequences of saying no, he ended up quietly paying the race tax.

Representing All *Black People*

When black faculty members are few and far between in a department, college, or university, it is commonplace for white faculty to repeatedly turn to these individuals and expect them to be the voice for all black people. Consequently, many black faculty who are in a solo situation (with few or no other black colleagues in their department) often feel the pressure that any view they espouse will be taken as being representative of all "the black community," "black America," or at a minimum, "the black population at _____ College." The potential to have your personal views applied so broadly can be stressful and make it difficult at the outset for you to feel comfortable in expressing and asserting yourself publicly as an individual.

Like any other racial group, black people in the United States have varied opinions and attitudes; consequently, no single individual can be realistically expected to represent all of the views that exist among the collective. Commonly, white faculty, students, and administrators hang on to the views expressed by one black faculty member and interpret these as group representations. This often is unconscious, but still results in the essentialist reduction of complexity into oversimplification. By taking a viewpoint advocated by one black faculty member and then generalizing it to all blacks, some white colleagues consider themselves educated, aware, and informed without having to invest energy into seeking out additional viewpoints and perspectives.

Carla was the only African American faculty member in an eight-person Department of Biology at a midsize private university in the Northeast. During a meeting that consisted of the entire College of Natural Sciences, there was a discussion about potential ways to improve the diversity of the student body. The debate quickly shifted to whether recruitment strategies should be based on targeting racial diversity or socioeconomic diversity. As the only black faculty member in the room, Carla could feel people waiting for her to weigh in on the debate. Having listened to her colleagues' arguments, Carla decided to express her strong belief that the college should continue to focus on race explicitly in order to attract students of color and she explained why. She was shocked, however, when one of her colleagues responded by saying:

> I'm just surprised to hear you say that, Carla. Just the other day I talked with Thomas Meyers, who as you know is an African American faculty member in the English Department, and he said that we should focus our efforts on students' class background because otherwise we are just attracting wealthy African Americans. He thinks that any of these affirmative action types of initiatives just privilege the affluent and leave poor people out in the cold.

Carla was stunned by her colleague's comment because, as she later explained, "Who cares what Thomas Meyers or anyone else thinks. I was voicing *my individual* opinion." But this incident was a reminder that, within a predominately white context: (1) almost anything that Carla said would be taken as being reflective of all other black people; (2) she would be sought out for comment on any issue even remotely having to do with race because of her visibility and solo status; (3) any individual opinion she expressed may be repeated as evidence of what "black people think"; and, (4) for all of these reasons, she would have to be intentional about her opinions in meetings and casual conversation.

Negotiating Belonging with Diplomacy

One of the most painful indignities resulting from the combination of the scarcity of black faculty and the disproportionately high number of black people in low-wage service positions on college campuses is that you may regularly be mistaken for a janitor, food delivery person, waiter, support staff, homeless person who has wandered onto campus, or a person in some other stereotypical role that is the only way some white people can make sense of your presence on their campus. When it happens once, it will feel like a simple and unintentional mistake. When it happens repeatedly, you may recognize the patterns that underlie the regular mistaken identification. By the 100th time, it becomes an annoying aggravation.

Sharon was a young black social scientist working at a large research-intensive university. Sharon's department had scheduled a faculty meeting during the first week of classes in the fall and she could not wait to attend her first "real meeting" in her first "real job." Because of a delay in making her campus office available, Sharon had been working at home and had little contact with other faculty prior to the meeting. She was especially excited to meet the faculty she had communicated with via e-mail but had not been able to meet face-to-face during her campus visit the previous year. When Sharon arrived at the conference room, only a few other faculty were there and none were people she had met during her interview. Feeling excited, she greeted the first person she saw with a warm smile and friendly "hello." The colleague, a sixty-something white male, looked up briefly and said, "You can put the sandwiches over there" while pointing toward an empty table, and went on unpacking his briefcase. Taken aback, Carla replied, "I don't have any sandwiches." The colleague was totally unfazed, and asked, "Then, what can I do for you? We're about to start our faculty meeting." At this point, although Sharon felt agitated, she calmly replied, "Hi, I'm your new colleague Sharon Jones. I work here."

While Sharon's colleague was horrified by his assumptions and apologized profusely after realizing his mistake, the message had been sent loud and clear: most black people on this campus work in a service capacity so, if I don't know you and you are standing in a room, you must be here to serve me in some way. Had this been the only time Sharon experienced mistaken identity, she could have chalked it up to an individual mistake. However, throughout her first semester, Sharon was repeatedly assumed to be a student, secretary, maid, or anything *but* a professor. The last straw came when a student seeking an override into her course the next term knocked on her open door. Even though she was the only person in the room, dressed in her most professional suit, and her name was clearly marked on a nameplate, the student said, "Excuse me, I'm looking for Professor Jones. Do you know where I could find her?"

Classroom Hostility

While institutional interactions reveal the intersection of race and power in academic organizations, it is often the interactions and incidents that occur in college classrooms where racism most clearly and immediately manifests for new black faculty. On predominately white campuses, students are unaccustomed to seeing a black person in a position of authority, much less teaching in a college classroom. It is this lack of experience with black professors that can lead white students to ask questions about your credentials ("Do you have a PhD?" "*You're* the professor?"), your professional experience ("Have you ever taught this class before?"), and—in courses where race is part of the content—objectivity and validity of the course content ("Are you just saying that because you're black?").

Because blackness is stereotypically associated with intellectual inferiority, students experience dissonance when they see a black person behind the podium. This results in an unconscious stance where the black professor must prove his or her credibility, intelligence, and experience to the students in the class and where the slightest perceived error will be read as incompetence. White students regularly critique the competency of black faculty as teachers, challenge their authority aggressively in the classroom, question their legitimacy as scholars, fail to show the most basic level of respect, and express overly familiar communication styles and greetings (as if interacting with a peer). Although general standards of decorum and classroom civility are on the decline throughout US college classrooms, the disrespect and aggressive nature of classroom hostility faced by black faculty differ in both frequency and tenor from those experienced by white faculty and are grounded in a deep sense that a black faculty member must prove his or her competency in the classroom, as opposed to being given the benefit of the doubt that is so readily extended to white male faculty.

In addition to the general questions of competence and differential treatment, white students may feel far more comfortable exercising their power over you as a black faculty member than over your white colleagues. This can take the form of going "over your head" to complain about your teaching to a higher authority figure such as a department head or dean (who is typically white and male). Students may also attempt to exert their power through end-of-semester evaluations where they critique black faculty more harshly, are less tolerant of black faculty who are tough in grading and strict with discipline, and are more likely to penalize black professors for being academically rigorous (particularly in courses where race relations are part of the course content).

In contrast to the disrespect of white students, black faculty can quickly become overwhelmed by students of color who desperately seek mentoring and guidance from a faculty member who might actually understand something about their experience. Because black junior faculty not long ago were students themselves, most remember their own experiences as a racial minority student at a predominately white institution. Specifically, they remember what it was like to see precious few faces of people who looked like them in front of the classroom and the silent, but powerful, message that the scarcity of black professors sends about blacks in academe. As a result, it is easy for black faculty to empathize with students who hope to forge a connection with them and sincerely want to serve in some supportive capacity. At the same time, there is a limit to what you can provide without putting yourself at risk by taking on more than you can reasonably handle (which quickly leads to burnout and resentment) or turning students away (which generates guilt).

Mosi was a 26-year-old African American anthropologist at a small liberal arts college. In Mosi's first month on the campus, he had been called a racist by a white student who made a scene and left his class, he had hung his diplomas on his office wall because he was so tired of students asking whether or not he had a degree, and his department chair had received student complaints about his "strict policies." During the same period of time, Mosi had been asked to become the faculty adviser for two different black student clubs, had met individually with scores of black students who had heard about his hire and wanted to meet with him, and had been invited to speak at the school's Fall Parents Weekend event to highlight the college's diversity.

Mosi's phone just kept ringing off the hook. Despite the fact that he had no experience in diversity training, the Residence Life staff asked him to provide three Asian students with private individualized diversity training as part of their punishment for using the "N" word at a dorm function. This was in addition to a request by the Admissions Office for Mosi to star in its new recruitment video in an effort to attract more students of color to the college. These, of course, were only the things Mosi had said yes to. There were many other service requests that he turned down immediately. While nobody intended to create the situation of service overload for Mosi—each of the requests seemed reasonable in and of itself and came from different units on campus—it was the cumulative effect of the time that Mosi was spending on them that prevented him from accomplishing any research or writing. But given the hostility he faced in the classroom twice a week, Mosi also felt the need to serve the students who respected him and to develop positive relationships with campus staff and administrators to offset the complaints about his teaching.

Racially Based Double Standards

Academe is fraught with racially based double standards that power-fully influence decisions about hiring, salaries, raises, promotions, and tenure—although it is rare for it to be explicitly articulated or openly ac-knowledged. A common manifestation of racially based double stan-dards exists with respect to expectations. White faculty tend to harbor lower and more negative expectations of black colleagues than of their white colleagues. While often unconscious, differential expectations are usually tied to the premise that blacks are less intelligent and less com-petent than their white counterparts. There are various ways that lower expectations can infiltrate colleges and universities, including:

- Discouraging black faculty from applying for highly competi-tive and prestigious positions, or not nominating them for awards, regardless of their actual level of qualifications and accomplishments.
- Making seemingly complimentary remarks about how a black colleague is "articulate" or "well spoken" (the unstated implica-tion being that, despite having an advanced degree, the presence of verbal skills is surprising and noteworthy).
- Writing evaluations, review letters, or letters of recommendation that emphasize different abilities (focusing on a white person's research skills and scholarly potential, but emphasizing a black person's teaching skills, work with students, and service as a role model and mentor to students of color).

During reviews and evaluations, racially based double standards can lead decisionmakers to emphasize deficits for black faculty while em-phasizing strengths for white faculty. Whether it is in the annual review or in tenure and promotion decisions, committee members (who are al-most always white) are more likely to focus on what black faculty are missing or have failed to do well enough, but to emphasize more of the accomplishments and assets of white faculty. For example, in evaluating two junior faculty for their third year review at a small liberal arts col-lege, the all-white committee noted that both junior faculty had positive teaching evaluations and two journal publications. In an effort to evaluate the candidate's progression toward tenure and promotion, the white junior faculty member was praised for having sole-authored her publications. What they did not discuss, however, was the fact that one of her publications was a brief research note that was only four pages in length. For the black faculty member, the discussion centered on the fact that her publications were coauthored with her former dissertation adviser. This was described as a concern and framed as a weakness ("It's not clear what her contribution to the articles are." "How do we know whether this is her work or the senior person's work?" "She doesn't seem to be developing independently as a scholar."). What was never acknowledged was that she was first author on one article and that both articles were of greater depth, length, and substance than the other junior faculty member's publications.

Racially based double standards also result in differential interpretations of similar behaviors among black and white faculty. For example, white faculty with coauthored publications are more likely to be positively described as "collaborative" while black faculty are more likely to be labeled as "dependent." When black faculty are recognized for their strengths as teachers, this often implies that they are less skillful as researchers, whereas the same connotation is less often attributed to white faculty. While serving on committees, white faculty are more likely to be recognized for their contributions, but black faculty are more likely to be criticized for "not pulling their weight" or they are accused of "doing too much service" to the neglect of scholarship. Nonacademic experiences for white faculty are often defined as good citizenship and as having a "well-rounded approach," but for black faculty the attribution is more likely to be one of being "distracted," "trying to be an activist," and being "not focused" on relevant responsibilities.

Racially based double standards also establish different rules regarding what is considered "acceptable conduct" for white versus black faculty. These rules, which are invisible yet silently understood, encourage white people to act assertively on their own behalf while discouraging blacks from doing the same. The double standard around what constitutes acceptable conduct for whites and blacks is rooted in a long history in the United States where white power has been aggressively maintained by limiting, controlling, and containing black people. For centuries, the white power structure has been threatened whenever black people have dared to display boldness, acted decisively on behalf of their interests, asserted themselves with authority and confidence, and refused to acquiesce to attempts to control them. Historically, whites have dealt with their sense of threat through explicit violence.

In more recent times, the threat that black empowerment poses to white power has been dealt with more subversively. One way is by labeling the same behaviors by whites and blacks in dramatically different ways. To intimidate and discourage black empowerment within colleges and universities, black faculty who behave in ways that convey a sense of entitlement, boldness, and authority are labeled "arrogant," "aggressive," "threatening," and "demanding." And blacks (as well as white women) are punished for not knowing their "proper place." Conversely, these same behaviors by white male faculty are labeled as "self-confident," "assertive," "goal oriented," and "leadership traits," and are subsequently rewarded.

Persistent Stereotypes

Numerous racially based stereotypes persist about black people and these tend to shape cross-racial interactions in two primary ways. The first is that many whites have internalized stereotypes about blacks that subtly shape and control how they perceive and interact with black people. White stereotypes define black people as deviant, different, exotic, excessively weak, threateningly aggressive, immoral, angry, intellectually inferior, and unable to meet basic social or academic requirements. The sheer number and negativity of black stereotypes distinguish the group from other groups on campus. At the same time, the negative stereotypes of blacks are also more dehumanizing and more focused on the very worst aspects of humanity. These stereotypes and their influence on how people view and treat blacks usually operate on an unconscious level. Nevertheless, the influence that stereotypes have on how white students, faculty, and administrators treat black faculty cannot be overemphasized.

A white female administrator at a large research university (who was widely viewed by campus administrators as the point person on diversity) wrote a grant on balancing work and family. She sought funds to support institutional programming that would address this issue at her institution, which sorely needed an intervention. The funder had asked that all proposals address "diversity," and the administrator wrote that the programs would especially assist African American faculty because so many of them were single parents. One of the committee members asked the administrator how she could reconcile this assertion with the data that showed that less than 20 percent of black faculty had children and all of them were married. The administrator quickly adjusted the language in the grant proposal, but it had already revealed her deeply embedded stereotype that black faculty are more likely to be single parents and struggling. Her assumption was so salient that she felt no need to confirm the information by checking it against readily available institutional data.

The second way that stereotypes shape life in the academy is that, over time, black faculty can become so accustomed to white students, colleagues, and administrators interacting with them in stereotypic terms that they become conditioned to anticipate such reactions at all times. Black faculty can come to a point of being constantly on guard for any sign of disrespect. In fact, during cross-racial interactions, many black people have an invisible antenna that scans the interaction for signs of being negatively viewed and treated by white people. Having been disrespected so many times before, black faculty ultimately learn to be on guard against mistreatment from whites and this makes them quick to pounce on any situation that runs the risk of turning into a racial slight.

The problem is that, in some cases, the negativity that appears to be present in a given interaction may not be related to race, but rather is due to some other issue entirely. As a result, the quintessential questions facing black faculty at all times are: (1) Was this slight racial? (2) Should I say something about it? (3) What will the consequences be? and (4) If I do choose to say something, what should I say and how should I say it? Because white faculty are not racially oppressed, they do not have to grapple with the dilemma raised by this series of questions. Therefore, they often fail to understand what it is like for black faculty who are constantly faced with having to wonder (and rarely be certain in absolute terms) what role race is playing in a given interaction. Although it should go without saying, the constant calculus of determining how to interpret an interaction, anticipating the consequences of action or inaction, and deciding whether and how to respond is intensely fatiguing over time. It is the cumulative stress of working in a hostile environment and experiencing daily devaluation and disrespect that can lead to the common feelings of "battle fatigue" among black faculty.

Exclusion from Networks

As if it were not hard enough to be a numerical minority within a department and institution, many black academics face the hardships of both intentional and unintentional exclusion from social networks that are critical to their professional success. Exclusion occurs when black faculty are not invited to participate in the informal social spaces where information is exchanged pertaining to teaching, external funding, grants and fellowships, and publishing collaborations and opportunities. Participation in these informal networks is an essential component of progress toward tenure and promotion because information and contacts flow through network connections, without which an individual faculty member is left on his or her own. Because most senior faculty in the United States are white, these informal social circles are also predominately white. Without a sponsor (a colleague who uses their power to help you), it can be difficult for black faculty to tap into these opportunity structures and resources. The frequency with which white faculty fail to include black faculty in informal social circles contributes greatly to feelings of exclusion and isolation.

Too often, black junior faculty in their first academic position attend to the explicit expectations of teaching and research, unaware that they are embedded in an implicit and unspoken political environment that will impact their promotion and tenure. Their numerical underrepresentation may feel isolating but, when they are not included in the informal networks and information sharing, it has a concrete and negative impact on productivity.

The subtleties of interpersonal communication represent another common way in which black faculty experience exclusion and isolation. Examples of exclusionary or alienating communication include:

- White faculty frequently interrupting or cutting off a black speaker.
- White colleagues ending a conversation when a black colleague approaches.
- White speakers failing to acknowledge comments made by black speakers.
- White speakers dismissing or denigrating remarks by black speakers about racial inequality.
- White speakers conveying contempt or hostility toward black speakers through nonverbal gestures (e.g., rolling one's eyes, grunting, gasping, aggressive pen tapping).

Black faculty may also experience exclusion and alienation through the allocation of resources, or the lack thereof. It is not uncommon, for example, for black faculty to be paid lower salaries than white faculty of comparable qualifications, to receive smaller raises, and to be awarded lesser amounts of professional development funds than white faculty. They also are more likely to be assigned less desirable offices (or asked to share offices), more likely to be denied time off for research or sabbatical requests, and less likely to receive graduate student assistants despite being more likely to be assigned to teach large undergraduate courses. When black faculty are provided fewer resources and receive them less frequently than their white peers, it not only feeds feelings of exclusion and alienation, but also has a concrete detrimental impact on productivity.

The Curse of Color Blindness

In the post–civil rights United States, race is one of the most volatile topics of conversation in the academy. While open dialogues about race often occur within racial groups, honest discussion about race rarely occurs in cross-racial settings. Whites fear that anything they say about race in the company of people of color will be used to label them as racist, and blacks fear that calling attention to racial insensitivities and injustices will cause white people to be defensively dismissive and accuse them of being "hypersensitive," "angry," or "paranoid."

White faculty frequently react to black faculty concerns that involve race by claiming color blindness. Assertions of "not seeing color" in a social world that is organized around race are absurd. We all see color and have been socialized to associate it with various personality traits and characteristics. Although it is biologically true that "we are all human," these types of assertions are most commonly used as a way to dismiss and de-emphasize the concerns of black faculty or for expanding the definition of diversity so far that white men can claim underrepresented status based on their political opinions, geography, or religion ("We're all oppressed."). In this way, racism becomes irrelevant and precludes a direct dialogue about race, but the manifestations of racism in black faculty members' lives persist.

The failure to engage in open, honest cross-racial dialogue stands as a barrier between white and black academics. As long as silence about racial issues remains the norm, academe will never truly be a welcoming and supportive environment for black faculty. The proverbial unacknowledged elephant in the room communicates to blacks that they are in a setting where the rules around race are "business as usual." In other words, their institution is a place where white power dominates and where black people must endure racial slights and inequalities in silence and isolation, or pay the price of speaking out. The unwritten prohibition against open discussions about race communicates that white faculty are largely uninformed about the complexities of race and are unwilling to be accountable for their racial privilege. Consequently, the failure to engage in open cross-racial conversations protects white power and undermines a spirit of racially progressive engagement.

Devaluation and Marginalization of Scholarship

Last, but certainly not least, if you are doing intellectual work that is in any way outside of your discipline's mainstream, you should be prepared to experience devaluation and marginalization. In other words, if your work pushes boundaries epistemologically, methodologically, disciplinarily, or politically, you will face an army of gatekeepers invested in maintaining the dominant ways of knowing, prevailing methodologies, high disciplinary walls, and the distribution of power in your institution. Not all black faculty are engaged in radical scholarship, and there are certainly fields where the dominant paradigms are so entrenched and uncontested that the term does not even make sense. However, of all the areas previously described where black faculty experience racial differences in their tenure-track experience, it is those who are engaged in radical intellectual projects who face the steepest climb toward promotion and tenure because theirs is not only a journey of navigating racial barriers, but a true battle against a Eurocentric epistemology that legitimizes some truth claims and systematically invalidates others.

Within higher education, the processes of knowledge validation are controlled by tenured faculty, administrators, journal editors, editors of academic and independent presses, grant reviewers, and credentialing bodies. As a junior faculty member, you are dependent on their validation of your work through the awarding of external funds and fellowships, publication of your research, and, ultimately, your promotion and tenure. The vast majority of people who will be determining the value of your scholarship are white men whose evaluations of the validity of your lines of inquiry, methods of study, and truth claims must pass through the filter of their own group's political interests. Consequently, faculty who ask research questions, utilize investigatory methods, and make truth claims that are not consistent with Eurocentric patriarchal epistemology and do not reinforce the status quo are likely to be ostracized, marginalized, or dismissed as irrelevant.

Certainly, not every individual who occupies a position of power is white and male and, for that matter, not all white men who are in positions of power see their interests as aligned with the ruling elite. Among the Eurocentric patriarchal sphere of power, some women and people of color are elevated to positions of power, but only because it is understood that they will align themselves with the interests of those already in power. Similarly, not all white men are committed to the interests of their group and, as such, they are unlikely to advance within institutional systems. What is important to bear in mind is that we are discussing the patterns and interests of groups and, within all groups, individual variations and exceptions exist.

The challenge facing black faculty who are engaged in scholarship that calls into question the academic status quo, mainstream research in their discipline, or the distribution of power in our society is that their values and interests are not aligned with the powers that be. This means that, if they dare to pursue lines of inquiry, utilize investigatory methods, and make truth claims that are not consistent with "mainstream" work in their discipline, they will be at risk of having their work discredited, delegitimized, and dismissed. Faculty whose research is applied, action oriented, engaged, or public or community based are likely to be labeled "nonacademic," "activists," and "unscholarly." So also are those who conduct qualitative research, value oral and visual presentations of scholarship, own their subjectivity, validate the expertise of everyday people, integrate reason with emotion, value personal expressiveness, employ humanizing dialogue, and concretize concepts by representing the lived experiences of the research participants they study. Because such work challenges Eurocentric patriarchal epistemological assumptions, it is often viewed as threatening to established traditions. Consequently, this type of research can be difficult to publish in mainstream referred journals and, even when published, can be viewed by tenure and promotion committees with skepticism, scorn, and questions over why the faculty member is not publishing in the top journals in his or her field.

Walter was in his third year on the tenure track as an assistant professor in the School of Allied Health. During a meeting with his department chair to review his midtenure progress, Walter was relieved to be affirmed for his excellent teaching, extraordinary service, and the fact that he had completed five single-authored publications. He was distressed, however, when his chair commented that the number of his publications would be offset by the fact that they appeared in second-tier and specialty journals that were perceived to be lower in quality than the discipline's flagship journals. Walter explained to his chair that the nature of his research was such that the top three journals were unlikely to accept his work, not because it was of lesser quality, but because his epistemological assumptions and research methods challenged the disciplinary status quo. For example, a large component of Walter's research focused on understanding the perceptions that existed among residents of a large low-income, predominately African American community about a massive diabetes education and management program that had been implemented in an effort to combat the high rates of the disease within this community. Walter's research was grounded in phenomenology and liberation theory that defines truth in relative terms, recognizes the role that power plays in shaping truth and reality, and centers the realities of the research participants. He used ethnography to gather his data, which he analyzed using grounded theory and qualitative methods.

As a qualitative researcher, Walter was not interested in what the statistics would reveal about his subjects. Instead, he was sensitive to the ways that the members of the community he was studying had been exploited by researchers and how they were wary and skeptical of "university types" who wanted to poke and prod them while offering little in return. Thus, he wanted his research to center the voices of his subjects and refused to utilize an epistemological framework that would not demand that he locate his role within his research and own his human subjectivity. In short, Walter's work was radical, and this constrained the choices of journals interested in publishing his work. Each time he submitted his manuscripts to the top journals in his field, he was rejected. Though no one ever said that Walter's work was not rigorous, the comments from blind reviewers centered on their disagreement with his core assumptions. Journals that were known for publishing qualitative research and nondominant discourses were relegated to second-tier status, and were therefore "less rigorous."

Summary

We are frequently asked, "Why write a book just for black academics on the road to tenure? All faculty need that information!" We interpret this as a question about what is different between the experiences of black and white faculty on the tenure track. We hope this chapter has answered that question by clarifying the unique experiences of (1) isolation, alienation, and excessive visibility; (2) classroom hostility; (3)

racially based double standards; (4) persistent negative stereotypes; (5) exclusion from networks; (6) the curse of color blindness; and (7) devaluation and marginalization of radical scholarship. While the institutional one-down position of being a junior faculty member is a temporary and role-specific location for white faculty, it does not follow them beyond the walls of their particular ivory tower. For black faculty, however, the institutional one-down position is integrated with their social one-down position on the basis of race, both within and outside of the academic context.

As a black faculty member, you may find yourself managing the dual impact of racial discrimination and devaluation while also managing the indignities and challenges that accompany your status as a tenure-track faculty member. Now that we have outlined the most common ways that race and power interact to shape your experience as a new professor, let us turn to a discussion of how you can manage these dilemmas on your road to promotion and tenure.

Suggested Readings

Benjamin, Lois. (Ed.). (1997). *Black Women in the Academy: Promises and Perils.* Gainesville: University Press of Florida.

Berry, Theodora, and Nathalie Mizelle. (2006). *From Oppression to Grace: Women of Color and Their Dilemmas Within the Academy.* New York: Stylus.

Chesler, Mark, Amanda Lewis, and James Crowfoot. (2006). *Challenging Racism in Higher Education: Promoting Justice.* New York: Rowman and Littlefield.

Cooper, Tuesday. (2006). *The Sista' Network: African-American Women Faculty Successfully Negotiating the Road to Tenure.* Bolton, MA: Anker.

James, Joy, and Ruth Farmer. (1993). *Spirit, Space, and Survival: African American Women in (White) Academe.* New York: Routledge.

Moody, JoAnn. (2004). *Faculty Diversity: Problems and Solutions.* New York: Routledge.

Moses, Yolanda. (1989). *Black Women in Academe: Issues and Strategies.* Washington, DC: Association of American Colleges.

Sotello, Caroline, and Samuel Myers. (2000). *Faculty of Color in Academe: Bittersweet Success.* Boston: Allyn and Bacon.

Stanley, Christine A. (Ed.). (2006). *Faculty of Color: Teaching in Predominately White Colleges and Universities.* Bolton, MA: Anker.

3 | The Politics of "Fit"

LISA'S first faculty appointment was as an assistant professor of anthropology within the Humanities Division at Mason College, a small liberal arts college in the Deep South. She was the only African American faculty member and one of three women in the twenty-person division. Within her first few days at Mason, Lisa's department chair, Mitch, explained to her that one of the keys to faculty productivity at Mason was the rich network of collegial relations that facilitated collaboration on joint projects and provided an avenue for vital feedback, moral support, and encouragement. Lisa heard what Mitch was saying, but she could not imagine what his words actually meant until she began to interact with her colleagues. She quickly realized, much to her shock, that her colleagues all came to campus every day and spent considerable time in their offices with their doors wide open. She also learned that it was implicitly expected that faculty members eat their lunchtime meal in the faculty dining room several days each week.

All of this stunned Lisa. Because of her family background, Lisa operated with a high degree of independence and autonomy. In fact, Lisa preferred to spend minimal time at campus, opting instead to hunker down with her laptop in her home office where in isolation she was extremely productive. She was more comfortable working independently and was proficient at giving herself the motivation and encouragement she needed to persist on projects. Lisa immediately established a routine whereby she came to campus only to teach her classes, to meet with students during posted office hours, and to attend required meetings. She also was opposed to the idea of eating in the faculty dining room. Although she liked many of her colleagues, she simply was not

accustomed to the level of closeness and constant interaction that occurred among them. Neither did she share a similar desire for such sustained and sociable relationships. In short, Lisa was uncomfortable with
the level of intimacy and dependency that faculty at Mason exhibited.
Within a few months, tensions had built up between Lisa and her colleagues, who took offense at the fact that she spent minimal time in her
campus office and almost never ate in the faculty dining room.

The contrast in Lisa's and her colleagues' approaches to closeness
and distance was exacerbated by issues of race. As the only African
American faculty member in her area, and as only one of two African
American faculty at Mason College, Lisa felt more comfortable keeping to herself. Personally, she did not feel like she had much in common
with her colleagues. And she understood the Southern race rules well
enough to know that most white people would accept her only if she
wasn't "too black" in their presence. To Lisa, life just seemed easier if
she kept her distance. Lisa's white colleagues had no clue about how
awkward things might feel to Lisa as both a racial minority and one of
only three women in their division. This is not to say that race did not
inform how her white colleagues perceived the dynamic between Lisa
and themselves. To the contrary, some of their perceptions of (and reactions to) Lisa were very much racially informed but, for the most part,
this occurred unconsciously and outside of their awareness. For example, several colleagues referred to Lisa as "aloof," and their tone suggested that they expected her to be more "grateful" for their willingness
to include her socially. Although none of her colleagues named race, it
is difficult to overlook the role that racially based stereotypes and biases
played in how they perceived her.

To complicate matters, Lisa also was raised in a family and socialized in a graduate program where people openly expressed their opinions
and were amenable to negotiation and change. Thus, despite Lisa's sense
that the closeness among the faculty at Mason was strange, she was open
to negotiating a different way of interacting and expected a similar level
of willingness to negotiate from her colleagues. Unfortunately, Mason's
orientation toward change was not nearly as flexible and adaptable as
Lisa's. The system was decidedly rigid when it came to change, and, as
a result, each of Lisa's overtures to work out a mutually agreeable way
of managing the differences about closeness were rebuffed and, in some
cases, met with outright hostility and punishment. For example, after
Mitch informed Lisa that she needed to spend at least six hours each day
in her campus office with the door open, Lisa challenged him by asking
why this was necessary. Mitch clearly did not welcome her challenge

and, instead of answering her question, he closed down the lines of communication by saying, "It's my job to help you make it here, and let me be very clear, if that's going to happen, you need to start acting like this is a place you want to be. If you continue to isolate yourself and fail to communicate that you're part of the team, the team is going to oust you. Right or wrong, that's just the way it is here."

Lisa was incensed by Mitch's response. What angered her most was not that the two of them disagreed about how to be a team player, but rather that he had shut down the possibility of having a dialogue, or even a debate, as a way of negotiating their differences. She felt silenced by Mitch and forcefully pressured into behaviors that simply did not feel comfortable or make sense to her. Lisa was painfully caught in the gap between her **personal system orientation** and her **institution's organizational system**.

Understanding the Fit Between You and Your Institution

All colleges and universities are organizational systems and, to succeed in any system, it is necessary to clearly understand how the system functions and how you fit within that system in light of your personal system orientation. While there are similarities across different types of academic institutions, campus-specific organizational systems exist as unique entities. They are different from one another, and distinct from their individual component parts. One of the greatest tools that you can possess is a clear understanding of your college's or university's organizational system, including the qualities that constitute your institution's character and the dynamics that define how it operates. At the same time, it is vital to be aware of your personal system orientation because each of us has a system orientation that strongly influences the types of organizational system that we are most and least likely to succeed within. The greater your comprehension of your personal system orientation, the better equipped you will be to negotiate the dynamics of your organizational system.

Typically, the term "fit" is used to assess how a job candidate may integrate intellectually and interpersonally into the culture of a particular department. However, what we focus on here is not the hypothesized fit discussed in hiring decisions, but the actual fit between you and your current department so that you can assess the dynamics of that particular academic system and engage in the more difficult task of evaluating your personal system orientation. Understanding each of these two factors will help you to develop a framework for understanding the politics of fit between you and your institution, pinpoint potential minefields of conflict, and evaluate the core issues that underlie conflicts that may arise.

How Does Your University System Function?

The first step toward self-empowerment on the tenure track is an objective analysis of the system in which you are embedded. Every faculty member must clearly understand their college's or university's organizational structure and its rules of engagement. Failing to do so can result in disorientation, missed opportunities, isolation, and costly mistakes. Learning how your university system functions is not difficult, but it requires you to be proactive and take a step out of your immediate daily reality to think about your campus as a whole.

How Is My Institution Organized?

At the most basic level, new faculty will benefit from familiarizing themselves with the hierarchical and administrative structure of their institution. In particular, learn how departments are organized, how colleges are organized, and the overarching layers of administration that subsume them. When you step back from your department and think about your college as an organization, it will help you to ask important questions such as: What is my institution's mission? Do we have a strategic plan to serve as a roadmap for the immediate and long-term future? If so, what priorities for future development and growth are articulated in that plan? How do my unit and my research agenda connect to that plan?

As graduate students, we often were so wholly immersed in our own department and individual dissertation projects that we gave little thought to how our graduate institution functioned. We believed that our job was to do rigorous research, and there were other people out there to run things. Regrettably, too many of us carry this student perspective into our new role as a faculty member. In the transition from graduate student to junior faculty, we can become so immersed in teaching our courses, serving on committees, and trying to get our research program off the ground that we do not have time to consider what else is going on around us. To better assess how your school is organized, what it claims to do, where it is going, and who is leading it, we recommend the following:

- Obtain a copy of the organizational chart for your school and study the institution's structure, including who the decisionmakers are in your unit, college, and university.
- Read your college's or university's mission statement.
- See if your institution has a strategic plan and review it.
- Make a particular point to learn the names and faces of your dean, provost, and president or chancellor.

What Support Services Exist to Help Me Succeed?

It also is critical to seek out and familiarize yourself with the programs, policies, and resources that exist to support junior faculty. This includes programs such as New Faculty Orientation, Mentor Matching, a Center for Teaching and Learning; services to support grant writing; and the various professional development workshops offered by your institution. In addition to helpful programming, you will want to be clear about institutional policies that govern your work life, such as junior faculty sabbatical leaves and maternity or paternity leave. Finally, you will also want to seek out information about any and all "pots of money" that exist to support your research and teaching, such as travel funds, research seed money, internal fellowships, and teaching enhancement grants. It is imperative to have an overall view of what your institution has to offer you so that, when you are in need of a particular service or resource, you know where to go and who can assist you.

In addition to the programs, policies, and resources available for your professional development, we strongly recommend that you acquaint yourself with the mental health services offered by your institution. We fully acknowledge that there is a long-standing stigma against therapy in black communities that too often keeps people who could be helped by weekly attention to their emotional development from taking advantage of that benefit. However, please recognize that the first few years on the tenure track can be incredibly stressful, demanding, and lonely. No black faculty member should feel the slightest bit of shame about taking an hour per week to address all the stressors he or she is likely to face, particularly those described in Chapter 2. One of the best ways to cope with that stress is to set aside time weekly to process your emotions with a professional.

We understand that some of the disconnect that exists between the black community and therapy is rooted in the fact that psychotherapy has a long history of failing to recognize the role of social context in the everyday struggles faced by members of marginalized groups. As a therapist, Tracey can attest to the frequency with which therapists attempt to treat ecologically based problems with psychological solutions. As a result, when members of oppressed groups seek out therapy, they are not irrational for having a skeptical attitude. It is not unreasonable to doubt the extent to which therapists may overlook or misunderstand the role that broader social forces play in the anatomy of one's suffering. And yet, there are progressively minded, culturally attuned, oppression-sensitive therapists who understand the intersection between psychology and ecology, and we strongly encourage junior faculty to search for and retain the services of these professionals as needed.

All junior faculty should understand the support mechanisms that their institution offers, but black faculty more often report feeling isolated and unsupported due to their underrepresentation. Most institutions acknowledge that underrepresented faculty face particular challenges and some have instituted specialized programs to build community, combat isolation, and create a support network above and beyond the department level. These may take the form of campus-wide status committees, black faculty organizations, or underrepresented faculty mentoring programs. Increasingly, colleges and universities are hiring senior academic diversity officers, so it would be worthwhile to find out if your institution has a senior-level administrative point person who manages underrepresented faculty concerns (e.g., a vice provost of faculty diversity or vice chancellor of multicultural affairs). If so, locate that person's contact information and meet him or her as soon as possible. Information such as this will help orient you to your environment and guide you toward people with whom you want to start building relationships at the outset of your career (as opposed to seeking them out only if you have a problem). Most of this information can be obtained from the university's website or through conversations with your department chair. Even if some of the resources that are offered may seem trite or a waste of time, take advantage of whatever is made available to you. For example, if you are offered a New Faculty Orientation, do not skip it! Orientations typically are boring and poorly organized, and provide you with information you do not need while skipping information you do need. However, orientations are a great way to obtain the type of organizational information that we have recommended here and, more importantly, they are a great way to meet other new faculty.

What Are the Rules of Engagement?

While understanding the basic structure of your organization is important, you also need to know the rules of engagement in terms of both the *written rules* (e.g., the process and timeline for annual reviews, third year review, and tenure review) and the *unwritten rules* (e.g., people work in their offices eight hours a day, teaching does not matter, everyone acts like a particular faculty member is not crazy despite his propensity for wearing bedroom slippers to class). Additionally, you will need to learn the race rules (e.g., black faculty sit on extra committees, are responsible for mentoring all black students, and should never ever mention racism when it comes to departmental policies and procedures).

The written rules should be readily available to you, although you often must proactively seek them out. This can easily be done by requesting an orientation meeting with your department chair when you arrive on campus or finding out if your institution has a faculty handbook. The unwritten rules, however, must be learned from careful observation and subtle questioning. The race rules are equally understandable from observation, but also require a carefully trained eye to detect layers of subtlety. In short, you must learn to notice what is going on around you. Are most people in their offices on a daily basis, or do most people work at home? Are those who work at home demeaned? What are the dynamics at your first faculty meeting (e.g., who is really running things, who is allied with whom, who is barking mad)? Who talks to you like a child and who treats you like a colleague? What happens when the dreaded word "diversity" comes up in discussion? Although there are similarities across academic departments, there are also many institutionally specific differences that will be to your advantage to recognize as soon as possible.

What Is Your Personal System Orientation?

The original system in all of our lives is the family in which we grew up. The experiences we have in our families of origin significantly influence the types of organizational systems that we are most and least likely to succeed within. As a result, identifying your personal system orientation and understanding how this will impact your compatibility with your institution's organizational system is a vital aspect of ensuring your professional success. Reflecting back on the discussion of Lisa, clearly a large part of the gap between Lisa and her institution was rooted in their differing system orientations. Lisa was raised in a family that taught her to prefer social distance and autonomy as well as to be open to negotiation and adaptation. In contrast, Mason College was a system that highly valued closeness and interdependency and was resistant to negotiation or change. For Lisa to manage the gap that existed between her colleagues and herself, she would first need tools to help her assess and conceptualize these respective orientations as a starting point for making informed decisions about how to address the differences effectively.

We rely on David Olson's (1989) circumplex model of family functioning as the basis for identifying personal system orientation. Olson conceptualizes the dynamics in our families of origin along two key dimensions of family functioning: **cohesion** and **flexibility**. Both of these dimensions vary within families and, as a result, exist on a continuum. Cohesion refers to the degree of closeness a family system manifests. At one end of the continuum, family systems are highly disengaged, meaning there is little closeness among family members. At the other end of the continuum, family systems are overly enmeshed, meaning that family members are too close and excessively connected. Either extreme is problematic; therefore, those families that are better able to balance separateness and connectedness are healthier. Flexibility refers to the degree to which family systems are open to change and capable of adapting to life circumstances. At one end of the continuum, family systems are extremely rigid, meaning they are closed to change. At the other end, family systems are chaotic, changing constantly and lacking stability and order. Again, both extremes are problematic because the more a family system is able to balance stability and change, the healthier it is.

To more easily conceptualize the important concepts portrayed by Olson's circumplex model, Figure 3.2 provides a visual illustration (see p. 42). This representation depicts the dimensions of flexibility and cohesion as opposing axes. Families can fall into one of sixteen possible categories that exist within one of three possible ranges. In the most extreme range, there are four possible types of families. In the midrange, there are eight possible family types that reflect families who are extreme on one dimension, but balanced on the other. Finally, within the center range, there are four possible types of balanced families: flexibly connected, flexibly cohesive, structurally connected, and structurally cohesive. Families that fall within the balanced range are the healthiest because they are stable yet able to change, and they balance the forces of separation and connection.

Cohesion

There are several characteristics that are associated with the dimension of cohesion, including the degree of separateness/togetherness, dependence/independence, "I-ness" versus "we-ness," loyalty, and time spent together. Where a family falls on the continuum of cohesion is reflected in how the system manifests these characteristics. For example, a **disengaged family system** is one where there is a high degree of separateness, a strong sense of independence and I-ness, a dearth of loyalty, and members spend very little time together. In an **enmeshed family system**, there typically is a high degree of connectedness, a high degree of dependence and we-ness, strong loyalties, and family members spend a great deal of time together. Family systems that are balanced in terms of cohesion reflect a mix of separateness and togetherness, interdependence, a mix of I-ness and we-ness, moderate loyalty, and family members spend some but not most of their time together.

Flexibility

Several characteristics are associated with the dimension of flexibility, including style of leadership, approaches to discipline, degree of negotiation, stability of roles and rules, and openness to change. Where a family falls on the flexibility continuum is determined by how it manifests these characteristics. For example, in an extremely **rigid family system**, we find an authoritarian leadership style, the use of forceful approaches to discipline, limited negotiation, clear and stable roles and rules, and minimal change. Conversely, in an extremely **chaotic family system**, we find a dearth of leadership, limited approaches to discipline, constant negotiation and discussion, dramatic shifts in roles and rules, and considerable change. Systems that are balanced with regard to flexibility reflect an **authoritative style** of leadership, democratic approaches to discipline, willingness to engage in some discussion and negotiation, clear and stable roles and rules that can be adapted, and moderate change.

Given the multitude of things that new faculty need to consider when starting their first tenure-track job, you may be asking, Why should I spend time thinking about the family system in which I grew up? Quite simply, the reason is that the type of family system in which you grew up profoundly shapes the person you have become and your system orientation. It shapes your core assumptions, what you consider to be "normal," and your expectations for social interactions. The dynamics in your family of origin in terms of cohesion and flexibility influence how you will function within various types of academic systems. Therefore, it is critically important to understand the type of family system in which you grew up and how it shapes your current system orientation.

The discussion of Lisa revealed that she grew up within a structurally disengaged family system and therefore exhibited high levels of autonomy and independence. Consequently, she preferred to spend minimal time at campus and was most comfortable working in isolation, which allowed her to be most productive. Campus was merely a place where she taught her classes, met with students during posted hours, and attended required meetings. Moreover, the level of closeness and constant interaction exhibited among Lisa's colleagues did not feel normal to her, and it was not anything she desired for the future. Yet, she was open to considering another way of functioning. In her family of origin, there was always space for people to express different opinions, to debate and argue, and to adapt and change in ways that were mutually beneficial to everyone involved. Lisa's adult system orientation (which was shaped by experience in her family of origin) was structurally disengaged and therefore different from her college's system orientation.

In contrast to Lisa, Mason College was a rigidly enmeshed system. The faculty at Mason had extremely close relationships and spent the majority of every workday on campus. In addition to their work, the faculty shared social relationships. Mason was also a system that was not terribly open to change. The college's policies, procedures, and culture had been the same for a long time and the system was solidly committed to doing things the way they had always been done. For this reason, there was little space for negotiation around other ways of conducting the institution's business and interactions.

How to Identify Your Personal System Orientation

You can use the circumplex model to gain insight into the type of family system in which you grew up, and take the first critical step toward understanding your adult system orientation and the impact it has on how you experience your current college's or university's system. To begin, focus on a period of time when you were growing up in your family that you believe was the most influential. Answer the questions in Figure 3.1 in the way that you think you most likely would have answered at that time. You should answer all of the Cohesion Questions and add the numbers corresponding to your responses together to get a total Cohesion Score, then answer the Flexibility Questions and calculate your total Flexibility Score. Next, plot your Cohesion Score and Flexibility Score on Olson's circumplex model (Figure 3.2) to determine where your family of origin is located. Knowing the type of family system in which you grew up is valuable information that you can

Figure 3.1 Cohesion and Flexibility Questions

Cohesion Questions

1. How much emotional closeness is there?

1	2	3	4
not close	generally close	very close	extremely close

2. How much emphasis on "I-ness" versus "we-ness"?

1	2	3	4
mostly I-ness	more I-ness vs. we-ness	more we-ness vs. I-ness	mostly we-ness

3. How much independence versus dependence is there?

1	2	3	4
very independent	more independent than dependent	more dependent than independent	very dependent

4. How much emphasis on loyalty?

1	2	3	4
minimal emphasis	somewhat emphasised	moderately emphasised	extreme emphasis

5. How often is free time spent together?

1	2	3	4
rarely	sometimes	often	very often

Total Cohesion Score _____

Flexibility Questions

1. What kind of leadership style prevailed in your family?

1	2	3	4
one person leads	sometimes shared	mostly shared	no clear leader

2. How much negotiation and discussion is there?

1	2	3	4
very little	occurs sometimes	occurs often	little ever resolved

3. How often do family members carry out the same roles around the house?

1	2	3	4
always	often	sometimes	rarely

4. How stable and clear are the rules in your family?

1	2	3	4
very stable and clear	fairly stable and clear	flexible and clear	change often and unclear

5. How much change is allowed to occur?

1	2	3	4
rarely	sometimes	generally open	very open

Total Flexibility Score _____

Figure 3.2 Olson's Circumplex Model

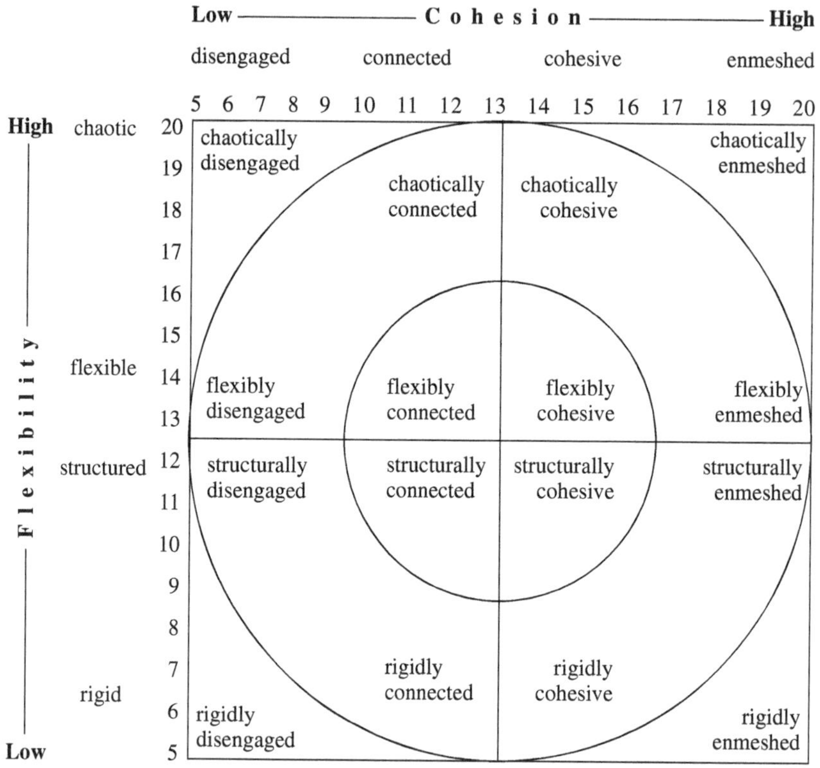

Low ——————————— C o h e s i o n ——————————— High

| disengaged | connected | cohesive | enmeshed |

Source: David Olson, Candyce Russell, and Douglas Sprenkle, *Circumplex Model: Systemic Assessment and Treatment of Families* (Binghamton, NY: Hawthorne Press, 1989).

use to better understand your adult system orientation and the types of institutional contexts you are most and least likely to succeed within.

A word of caution: there are no hard and fast rules affirming that, if you grew up in a particular type of system, you will absolutely react in certain ways to similar or dissimilar dynamics in adulthood. For example, someone who grew up in a rigidly enmeshed family system is likely to prefer highly authoritarian, hierarchical, controlled systems that demand loyalty and commitment to the organization (such as the military). On the other hand, that rigidly enmeshed family system might have been so alienating that, as an adult, this same person instead is quite reactive to similar systems, thereby displaying a strong preference for loosely structured systems that encourage a high level of autonomy, cre-activity, and independent activity. The point is that we make no claim that growing up in a certain type of family system will produce a specific system orientation in adulthood. We do claim that your family of origin strongly influences your personal system orientation. The more you understand the dynamics of your family of origin, the better equipped you will be to identify and comprehend your personal system orientation as an adult and recognize where your points of struggle reside with your institution's system orientation.

Academic Socialization and the Role of Graduate School

Inevitably, if you are reading this book, you have already experienced the ease or angst that flows from the fit between your personal system orientation and the system orientation of an academic institution as a graduate student. The program or department where you conducted your graduate work had a system orientation and, depending on your personal system orientation, you experienced degrees of compatibility or incompatibility during your graduate education. If there was a high degree of fit between your system orientation and the graduate program where you earned your degree, you most likely entered your first academic appointment with little thought about the issue of fit between you and your institution. However, if there was a poor degree of fit between your personal system orientation and the orientation of your graduate program, you very likely assumed your new role as a faculty member with some understanding of the importance of fit. Moreover, how you managed clashes between your system orientation and the orientation of your graduate program are important indicators of how you likely will respond to and negotiate any incompatibilities you may face as a new faculty member.

As a general rule, it is our contention that the personal system orientation you acquired from your family of origin is primary and almost always functions as a default. However, the experiences you had as a graduate student influence what you learn to expect from (and how to function within) an academic system. The system orientation of your graduate program played a role in shaping your system orientation as it pertains to academe. For example, the personal system orientation you acquired from your family may have been rigidly enmeshed; yet, if you were socialized in a rigidly disconnected graduate program, you may have learned to tolerate high degrees of closeness within an academic setting and this may, in fact, be your expectation as a new faculty member. If you then find yourself on the faculty of a university that is rigidly enmeshed, it may feel like a natural fit because it matches the experiences in your family, but it may not fit with what you have come to specifically expect from an academic system. Therefore, in addition to assessing the personal system orientation you learned from your family, it is worth devoting some thought to how your secondary socialization in graduate school may have affected your expectations and attitudes.

The Politics of Fit

Your personal system orientation will heavily influence the "goodness-of-fit" between you and the academic institution you are working within. If there is a high degree of compatibility between your personal system orientation and the dynamics of your institution, life will be infinitely easier for you than if there is a wide gap between your orientation and the institution's dynamics. In certain cases, if the gap between a new faculty member's personal system orientation and an institution's character is so wide that it cannot be traversed, a parting of the ways may be the best option. In most cases, however, there will be some combination of overlap and divergence between the personal system orientation and the organizational system's character. That is, in some ways, the new faculty member and the institution will be well suited to each other; in others, there will be clashes. Your greatest strength will lie in knowing where the alignments and the clashes reside so that you can make informed choices about how to handle particular situations.

There may be any number of issues about which you and your institution will disagree or be incompatible. These different viewpoints and ways of being are not a problem in and of themselves. Instead, the more critical issue is how flexible you and your institution will be toward resolving the conflict and change. Where you and your system rank on the flexibility continuum will be the key factor in whether or not you can make adjustments to your fit. It is one thing to disagree about how much time you should spend in your campus office versus your home office, or to disagree about whether it is acceptable to be asked to sit on all of the diversity-related committees. The key is whether or not you can discuss these differences and negotiate a mutually beneficial compromise. In other words, in flexible organizational systems, each party possesses some openness to considering the other's point of view and a willingness to entertain making changes. But when individuals who are high on flexibility exist in organizational systems that are inflexible, there can be a fundamental conflict. That leads us back to Lisa's case.

Lisa's personal system orientation was structurally disconnected and her institution's system orientation was rigidly enmeshed. As a result, each had divergent approaches to connection, space, closeness, and autonomy. And while Lisa's orientation made her amenable to negotiation and reasonable change, Mason (as a system) was far more rigid and unwilling to entertain adaptation and change. This was the core issue underlying the conflict or lack of fit between Lisa and Mason. Let us imagine for a moment that Mason had been more open to change. If, for example, Mason was a flexibly or structurally enmeshed (rather than rigidly enmeshed) system, negotiation around differences related to closeness and distance would have been possible. Both parties would have been open to making adjustments to each other's preferences around cohesion.

It is inevitable that substantive conflicts will arise between you and those who have power over you in your college or university. The presence of different opinions and standpoints is not what determines how well you and your system fit. The defining factor with regard to fit is the extent to which some degree of flexibility exists on each side. For your part, it is important that you strive to manifest a moderately flexible stance. If your system orientation is such that you are either extremely flexible or extremely rigid, it will be important that you work with yourself to find comfort on more moderate ground. Too much flexibility will make you so willing to accommodate and bend that you will be easily exploited, just as too much rigidity will inhibit you from making necessary compromises and adaptations.

In terms of your system, you are likely to find it difficult to fit with a system that is rigid and resistant to negotiating and compromising. Whenever differences arise within rigid systems, these systems will almost always expect you to surrender your position and to do all of the accommodating . . . period. Rigid systems respond to differences via domination. In other words, they will seek to overpower you into submission and, if you fail to submit, destructive conflict will likely erupt. The short-term consequences of this may be that you will decide you cannot tolerate being in a rigid system, and the lack of fit between you and the institution will be reason enough for you to leave. Alternatively, there may be reasons for you to stay and attempt to work it out. Although this will be challenging, there are strategies you can employ to negotiate conflict constructively. With the use of certain types of strategies, it may be possible to constructively work through and resolve dif-

ferences in mutually beneficial ways even in systems that are highly resistant to negotiation, adaptation, and change. An in-depth presentation
of and discussion about practical strategies for effectively handling conflict are the focus of our chapter on constructive conflicts (Chapter 9).

Suggested Reading

Olson, David, Candyce Russell, and Douglas Sprenkle. (1989). *Circumplex
Model: Systemic Assessment and Treatment of Families*. Binghamton, NY:
Hawthorne Press.

PART 2
Mastering Your Technique

4 | Tenure and Time Management

SCOTT was an assistant professor in the Medical School of a large research university. He was Ivy League educated, and had developed into a confident and well-respected surgeon. Scott was shocked and devastated to receive a lukewarm third year review. Although his department found his service and teaching excellent, they made it clear that his lack of publications and external funding was unsatisfactory. In no uncertain terms, Scott was told that he needed to publish ten to twelve articles, and secure external funding, in order to be promoted with tenure. When Scott came to see us, he confided that he had "many brilliant ideas," but had not actually tested them, much less completed any writing. Scott had been so caught up in the daily grind of surgery, teaching, and service that he had failed to give much thought to writing. He kept telling himself that, when he got a big block of time, he would sit down and write. But after the third year review, Scott felt panicked because of the short amount of time left until he came up for tenure. He knew he needed to start doing things differently, but was not sure *how*; he was increasingly thinking that he should convert his appointment to a clinical line and remove himself from the tenure track entirely.

Does Scott's situation sound familiar? We know many faculty like Scott: they are incredibly smart and capable people who get so involved in the chaos of day-to-day life that they lose track of the big picture. By the time they look up and figure out that they have failed to attend to long-term strategic thinking (this happens most commonly after a critical third year review), they are standing in a deep hole and trying to figure out how they can climb out of it. The Scotts of the academic world are operating on at least one (or a combination) of five common myths

49

about academic time management and it is their faith in these myths that has led them into crisis and in need of an intervention.

The Myths You Must Overcome

Myth 1: Six Years Is a Long Time

There is a pervasive myth among junior faculty that six years on the tenure track is a long time. In some ways, six years *is* a long time. It is a long time to be living on probationary status, a long time to be walking on pins and needles, and a long time to be uncertain about your future. Many people spent approximately the same amount of time in graduate school and that seemed like a hellish eternity. Given the drudgery and drama of the job market, many junior faculty feel such a tremendous sense of relief after obtaining their first faculty appointment that they mistakenly view their first year as one to "get settled in" to their new surroundings, focus on teaching, and relax a bit in their new status.

Reality check: "Six years is a long time" is a myth for two important reasons: (1) you actually have *five* years to prepare for tenure (not six); and (2) the publication process from submission to review, revision, and production is lengthy. We are regularly shocked to find that junior faculty do not realize they have only five years to prepare a tenure case. Your sixth year is the year when your packet will be under review; therefore, nothing that you do that year will count toward the support of your case. To be specific, most institutions start seeking external reviewers for your materials in the summer before your sixth year. Those outside experts will review your promotion packet in either late summer or early fall of your sixth year. Their reviews go to members of your departmental committee, who will meet and vote sometime during the fall semester. Depending on your institution, the vote will continue to move up the organizational hierarchy throughout the academic year, culminating in a confirmatory vote by your institution's Board of Trustees late in the spring of your sixth year. What this means is that you have from your first day of employment until the end of your fifth year to prepare your tenure case.

The second problem with the "six years is a long time" myth is the length of time required to take an article or book to publication. Depending on your discipline, the time from draft to publication of an article can be several years. Given the length of your probationary period, you will have to work very hard and very efficiently in order to meet the publication standards at your institution. As a result, it is essential for new faculty to hit the ground running on their research projects, develop healthy writing habits, and proactively create support systems from the outset of their academic career.

Myth 2: I Don't Need to Plan, I'm Brilliant!

Maybe because neither of us has ever thought of ourselves as "brilliant," we have been spared the miasma emanating from this particular myth. But many of the junior faculty with whom we have worked have expressed some version of the following:

> I have brilliant ideas, *lots* of them, and this makes me different than regular people who struggle to come up with a single good idea in their entire career. I have so many great ideas that I can afford to give some away. Someone should just follow me around with a tape recorder and laptop and record the ideas that fall out of my head. In fact, because I'm so brilliant, I shouldn't have to even engage in the mundane activities of conducting research and writing. But if I must, I will wait until I get an enormous block of free time. Then, it will be easy because I've already worked it all out in my head.

Reality check: It does not matter how smart you are, think you are, or have been told that you are—you still have to sit your butt down in a chair and write. Academic writing is tedious, slow, and agonizing work. For perfectly average people, it is work. For brilliant people, it is work. Articles take time to conceptualize and draft. Once an article is completed, obtaining feedback from others takes additional time. Considering their comments, making revisions, and submitting the article to a journal take even more time. That same article may wait two to twelve months for review by the journal's editorial board and, when it is returned, the process will start all over again (whether you are revising it for resubmission or submitting it to another journal). All of the brilliant ideas in the world are simply personal stimulation if they never are put to paper, published, and discussed by others in your discipline.

Myth 3: I'm a Fraud and Don't Deserve to Be Here

The "I'm a fraud" myth is the inverse of the "I'm a genius" myth (and sometimes lurks beneath the latter). In both cases, faculty members are not productive because of their flawed assumptions. But the frauds believe they are deficient in their fundamental intellectual abilities and have made it through the educational system only by some combination of luck and deception. Because of the inner belief that they are inadequate, the prospect of having their written work evaluated and critiqued is terrifying. This is rooted in deep insecurity and fear of failure and, to some extent, even fear of success (they may believe ultimate failure is inevitable). Because writing makes faculty vulnerable to exposure of their perceived and feared inadequacies, it becomes extremely difficult for individuals who hold this belief to commit to writing. Instead, they are more likely to focus on the day-to-day grind of teaching and service as a way of temporarily avoiding their fears and their writing.

Reality check: In today's academic job market, nobody who has a job is unqualified because there is a long line of people applying for each and every opening. Sometimes we have to ask ourselves why we refuse to believe that we are smart and deserving of success. For many black faculty, experiencing a lifetime of subtle devaluations and existing in a context of racist beliefs that black people lack intelligence can be major factors. Others have had to face indignities daily, constantly defend their ideas, and even prove the legitimacy of their presence on campus, which can exacerbate these insecurities. You can run for a while, but ultimately you cannot hide. At some point, you will have to produce written work, thereby placing your ideas in the public domain and risking the humiliation you so deeply fear. Or, perhaps you will effectively sidestep writing for so long that inaction will bring about the disgrace you feared all along, but in the form of criticism for failing to produce any publications and a resultant tenure denial.

If you harbor an inner belief that you are inadequate and unworthy, you must start by figuring out why. One of the best ways to overcome insecurities around your work is by sharing your ideas, presenting your work in progress, circulating drafts, and discussing emerging chapters or papers with others. This is what academics do, and it represents the core process of scholarly engagement.

Myth 4: I've Come This Far Without Planning, Why Start Now?

We concede that many an academic has made it through his or her undergraduate and graduate education without much long-term or strategic planning. Some people may even have been fortunate enough to land a tenure-track faculty position without any planning. Others stumble into research projects, book contracts, and invited chapters in edited volumes. Scott had never planned ahead and he had done just fine so far. After all, he was a successful surgeon who lived in a great city, and everyone in his personal life thought he was brilliant and successful.

Reality check: It is perfectly fine if you moved through your undergraduate and graduate programs with little planning, but you cannot count on that attitude to help you win promotion and tenure. This is because the constraints of being on the tenure track are unlike those of an undergraduate, a graduate student, or a candidate in the job market. Instead, you now have a fixed amount of time to be effective, after which you will be evaluated. In previous stages of your academic career, you could always take a year off, postpone graduation, or spend one more year in the job market. But once you are in a tenure-track position, the time constraint is externally imposed and, with few and politically costly exceptions, it is absolute. Ready or not, in your sixth year, you will be evaluated. Published or not, you will be evaluated.

Myth 5: I Don't Need to Plan Because I Have Lots of Free Time

We often think that, if the only things scheduled on our calendar are teaching and a few meetings, we do not actually need a calendar or to plan our time outside of those events. We can prepare for teaching sometime before class, and most meetings require only our attendance. The problem is that we forget to make time for research and writing. We forget that we need to sleep eight hours per night to be functional the next day. We forget that we need exercise, healthy relationships, leisure, and time to attend to the basic functions of our lives. We overestimate the actual time that we have, yet underestimate all that we need to accomplish in that time. Many of us hope that everything will "somehow just get done." The regrettable outcome is that too many of us end up compromising sleep for last-minute course preparation and sacrificing progress on long-term writing projects in favor of short-term teaching and service-related deadlines. The end result is that the quality of our interpersonal relationships, our publication record, and our long-term success as academics can be sacrificed to the "free time" myth.

Reality check: It is precisely because you have autonomy over your work and because you have a flexible schedule that it is easy to fall under the sway of the "free time" myth. The twin blessings of academic work are flexibility and autonomy, but these can be the greatest obstacles for many people because the reality is that writing does not just happen. Because your schedule is not superimposed on you by your institutional structure, and because you are responsible for organizing your time and pacing your productivity, it is easy to fall prey to the illusion that you have more time than you really do. If you are going to successfully win tenure, it is critical that, from the first day of your new academic position, you establish a realistic schedule and assume a disciplined approach to pursuing your scholarly production. If you don't do this, you will run the risk of ending up like the many junior faculty who seek our help in their third, fourth, or fifth year because they have no publications, their life is out of balance, and they are miserable.

Effective Time Management: Developing and Executing a Strategic Plan

Let us begin with a focus on getting your priorities straight. For a new faculty member, this means understanding that you have only five years to build your tenure case. To reiterate: your tenure packet will go out to external reviewers in the summer before your sixth year and that entire year you will be under review, so, whatever you are going to do, you need to do it in your first five years. These years will be tilted toward professional activities and it is important to know that, unlike any other time in your career, the first five years of a faculty appointment will dominate your entire life. We are not saying that this is healthy or ideal but only recognizing that it is the reality of life on the tenure track. This does not mean that nothing else can happen in your life, but try to make conscious decisions about other major decisions with the awareness that you will be under intense stress and scrutiny during those five years. Knowing that you have five years to build a tenure case means that you should create a five-year strategic plan for how you will get from your first year on the tenure track to the submission of a rock-solid promotion packet at the end of your fifth year.

In the remainder of this chapter, we will outline and discuss the five steps of strategic planning for new faculty. The steps we describe are essential to effectively managing your time, publishing prolifically, and winning tenure. The steps will provide you with a general planning process that you can use to develop and successfully execute your individual strategic plan. Importantly, these steps can (and should) be adapted according to your discipline, your ambition, and the promotion and tenure criteria at your institution. We will elaborate on each step below and provide illustrative examples of real faculty members who experienced success by following them. The five steps of strategic planning for new faculty are:

1. Identify your professional goals.
2. Outline the projects and tasks.
3. Map your projects onto time.
4. Execute the plan on a daily basis.
5. Create accountability and support.

Step 1: Identify Your Professional Goals

An effective strategic plan begins with a clear statement about your **goals**. Therefore, the first questions you have to ask yourself are: What are my professional goals? and Where do I want to be in five years? The answers to these two questions will not be the same for everyone. For example, Alisha's first job was at a community college and her primary goal was not to get tenure at that institution. Instead, her goal was to make herself marketable enough that she could move to a liberal arts college in a warm climate. Her friend and colleague Tim had completely different goals. He wanted to maximize his income (so he could travel) and minimize his stress. When the two of them talked about where they could see themselves in five years, Alisha imagined herself on the tenure track at a liberal arts college. Tim imagined himself teaching at the same community college but, importantly, with tenure and having moved five steps up on the pay scale so that he would be starting to receive his union-mandated "longevity" bonus.

The point is that it does not matter what your professional goals are; it matters that you are clear about them and that you *write them down*. Being conscious of your goals does not guarantee that they will be realized, but you are far more likely to achieve your goals if you are clear about them, commit them to paper, and follow the remaining four steps of strategic planning to actualize your goals. We will use Brenda's story as an example of this process.

Brenda was a new faculty member in the humanities at a small urban research university that had aspirations of improving its national ranking by raising research standards for tenure and promotion. Because her mother is a professor and her father is a college administrator, Brenda was particularly savvy about the need to develop an individual strategic plan at the start of her first year. Although Brenda was happy about the location of her college (in the city where she grew up and where her family still lived), she wanted to leave open the possibility of moving to a larger and more highly ranked institution if the opportunity arose. Following the first step of creating an individual strategic plan, Brenda identified the following five professional goals:

Goal 1. Transform her dissertation into a publishable book.
Goal 2. Publish two articles from her dissertation research.
Goal 3. Receive a one-year fellowship or postdoctoral fellowship.
Goal 4. Design and begin her second major book project.
Goal 5. Successfully win promotion and tenure.

Step 2: Outline the Projects and Tasks Necessary to Achieve Your Goals

Brenda had an ambitious set of goals for her strategic plan. While determining reasonable goals is an important first step, she also had to figure out how to accomplish her goals in practical terms. Specifically, Brenda had to identify the specific **projects** she would work on that would culminate in the achievement of each goal. For example, her first goal was to transform her dissertation into a publishable book manuscript. To meet this goal, she had to determine what projects would help her achieve it. Here is her list of the ten projects necessary to move her manuscript from a dissertation to a book:

Project 1. Write a draft book proposal.
Project 2. Ask trusted advisers how to transform the manuscript, and revise the proposal accordingly.
Project 3. Complete additional reading and research required for revision.
Project 4. Meet with editors at conferences to discuss the book or have sponsors help introduce the book to their editors.
Project 5. Revise the manuscript.
Project 6. Circulate the manuscript to trusted assessors to read and review.
Project 7. Submit the manuscript to an academic press.
Project 8. Make final revisions based on blind reviewers' comments.
Project 9. Prepare the manuscript for production.
Project 10. Edit the final page proofs.

The cumulative outcome of completing these ten projects will be the successful publication of Brenda's book. Once she had outlined the basic path to publication for her book—a path paved with ten separate projects—she could then step deeper into the process by asking herself what specific **tasks** were associated with each of the ten separate projects. For example, Brenda's first project was "write a draft book proposal." However, Brenda had never written a book proposal, was not clear what an effective book proposal would look like, and was not even certain where to begin. So we assigned Brenda the homework of imagining how she could break that project down into a manageable set of tasks. She determined that writing a book proposal is composed of the following ten tasks:

Task 1. Read a book on proposal writing.
Task 2. Ask colleagues for samples of successful book proposals.
Task 3. Read other people's successful proposals.
Task 4. Research potential academic presses.
Task 5. Research the market competition.
Task 6. Write the proposal.
Task 7. Revise the proposal.
Task 8. Ask others to read the proposal and provide feedback.
Task 9. Meet with others to discuss feedback.
Task 10. Make final revisions to the proposal for submission.

In order for Brenda to move forward in a concrete and manageable way, she had to understand the relationship among her goals, the projects necessary to achieve them, and the tasks associated with each project. The relationship among goals, projects, and tasks is critical for new faculty for several reasons (see Figure 4.1). First, we assign this homework to the faculty with whom we work individually, because it moves most of them out of a state of feeling paralyzed and overwhelmed by a big goal like "publish my first book." Publishing a first book is a common goal for faculty in the humanities, yet many do not have the slightest idea of how to go about achieving it. The second reason we assign this homework is that listing the projects and imagining the associated tasks demystify the process. In order to complete her homework, Brenda had to ask explicit questions of her colleagues (which she would not have done otherwise) and to learn how things get done (which reduced the anxiety of the unknown). In short, creating a strategic plan forced Brenda to proactively engage senior colleagues in her department and form the foundation of a mentoring relationship.

Third, in addition to identifying manageable projects and demystifying the overall process, we encourage new faculty like Brenda to outline

Figure 4.1 Moving from Goals to Specific Tasks

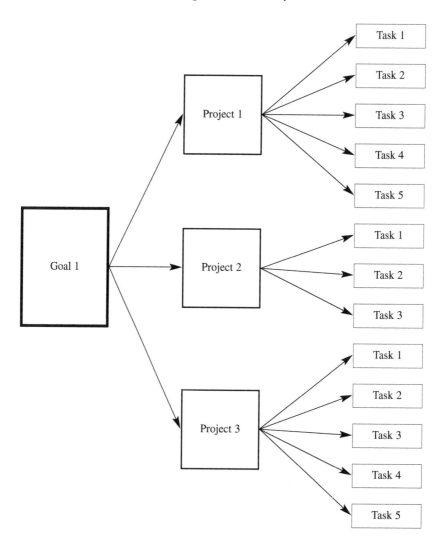

their goals, projects, and tasks because that is central to managing their time. The amount of time necessary to compete a project can be estimated only by listing all the associated tasks, figuring out how long it will take to complete each task, and then adding all the hours together to determine the total. Because one of the most common technical errors new faculty make is underestimating the total amount of time to complete a task, our rule is to multiply whatever you estimate by 2.5. We did not make up this rule. Kerry Ann learned it from one of the high-performing faculty members in her graduate program. However, we call it the **reality rule** because 2.5 seems to be the average factor by which work time is underestimated. Encouraging new faculty to multiply their estimates of task time by 2.5 has improved the overall quality and practicality of their strategic plans. Brenda's project management sheet for writing the proposal is shown in Table 4.1.

Because Brenda had learned how to map out the **tasks** involved in completing her first **project**, "write a draft book proposal," she could then go on to complete the same estimation process for each of the other **projects** that were necessary for her to meet her first **goal**: "transform my dissertation into a publishable book."

Brenda's case is a good example to walk you through the first two steps involved in developing and executing your own strategic plan: (1) identify your goals, and (2) outline the projects and tasks necessary to achieve your goals. Keep in mind, however, that we have outlined only one of Brenda's projects that made up one of her five goals. To complete her five-year plan, Brenda had to go through the same process for all five of her goals: (1) transform her dissertation into a publishable book, (2) publish two articles from her dissertation research, (3) receive a one-year fellowship or postdoc, (4) design and begin her next book project, and (5) win promotion and tenure. To view Brenda's complete strategic plan and other samples of individual strategic plans, log on to www.BlackAcademic.com and click on "reader-only resources."

Table 4.1   Project Management Sheet

Goal: Transform my dissertation into a publishable book
Project: Write a book proposal

Task	Number of Hours
1. Read a book or article on proposal writing	8
2. Ask colleagues for samples of successful proposals	2
3. Read other proposals	3
4. Research publishers	4
5. Research the market competition	4
6. Write the proposal	20
7. Revise the proposal	4
8. Ask others to read the proposal and provide feedback	1
9. Meet with others to discuss feedback	5
10. Revise the proposal	4
Total project time	55
Reality rule	× 2.5
Estimated project time	137.5

Step 3: Map Your Projects onto Time

Brenda's first **goal** was to "transform her dissertation into a publishable book." To do this realistically and show concrete progress so that she could have an impressive and successful third year review, Brenda knew that she could not wait until her second or third year to start making progress toward this goal. She also was conscious of the fact that she wanted to be marketable enough to move to a more highly ranked institution if she chose to go back on the market during her third year. Given all of these factors, Brenda decided to concentrate on the projects associated with her book in the first three years of her five-year plan. So when we challenged Brenda to map the **projects** associated with her goal onto a five-year timeline, her first outline looked like the following:

Year 1
- Seek input from trusted advisers about what needs to be done to transform the dissertation into a book manuscript.
- Write a book proposal.
- Complete any additional reading and research required.
- Meet with editors at conferences to discuss the book or have sponsors help introduce the book to their editors.

Year 2
- Revise the manuscript.
- Circulate the manuscript to trusted assessors to read and review.

Year 3
- Revise the manuscript.
- Submit the manuscript to a publisher.

Year 4
- Make final revisions based on external reviewers' comments.
- Prepare the manuscript for production.

Year 5
- Edit the final page proofs.

After mapping the projects associated with achieving Goal 1 (transform the dissertation into a publishable book) onto her five-year timeline, Brenda had to do the same with Goal 2 (publish two articles from her dissertation research), Goal 3 (receive a one-year fellowship or postdoc), Goal 4 (design and begin her second major book project), and Goal 5 (successfully win promotion and tenure). One of the most basic tenets of time management is to *start with your goals and work backward*. Developing a five-year plan from clearly defined goals will enable you to see what work you need to accomplish during each academic year.

Once you have estimated the time necessary to complete your projects, you will move from what needs to be done each year to planning the details of each semester and break schedule. In Brenda's case, she began her first year with the knowledge that she had to write a book proposal, a project that is composed of ten distinct tasks that would take her 137.5 hours to complete. Knowing this, she was able to further divide the tasks into semester work, as shown in Table 4.2.

For Brenda, breaking the project "write a proposal" into smaller, more manageable tasks both demystified the entire process and reduced her anxiety because none of the individual tasks was terribly difficult and she knew that the cumulative outcome of all the tasks would be a completed book proposal. Again, we have simplified this example by mapping just one project so that you can understand the process of moving from your five-year goals to a specific semester-by-semester work plan. It is difficult and time consuming to create your strategic plan, but it is well worth the investment. We can only imagine how differently Scott's third year review (described at the beginning of this chapter) might have ended if he had begun his first year on the tenure track with as clear a sense of his goals, projects, and tasks as Brenda had.

Table 4.2   Semester Work Plan

Fall Semester	Holiday Break	Spring Semester	Summer
Read a book or article on proposal writing	Research academic presses	Revise the proposal	Make final revisions to the proposal
Ask colleagues for samples of successful proposals	Research the market competition	Ask others to read the proposal and provide feedback	Submit proposal
Read other proposals	Write the proposal	Meet with others to discuss feedback	

Step 4: Execute the Plan on a Daily Basis

Time management is one of those things that academics often think does not apply to them. Time management is for people in business, people who have no autonomy over their work, people who work 9 to 5, people who have to maintain schedules, or people who have type A personalities. Given that academics tend to believe that we are utterly unique in the way that we work, and that the intellectual work we do defies all management strategies, many of us resist scheduling our reading, research, and writing and end up feeling frazzled, missing deadlines, and being overwhelmed.

Sabrina's story is typical of a new faculty member. A psychology professor at a large, urban research university, Sabrina felt like she was constantly running around, never had enough time, and ended most days feeling disappointed and frustrated by how little she had gotten done. Every week, she stayed awake until 4:00 A.M. the night before her graduate statistics seminar frantically preparing for the next day's class. With only a few hours of sleep, she dragged herself through the day and was barely alert during class time. Afterward, she would go home, crash, and end up sleeping until 10:00 A.M. the next day. The remainder of the week, Sabrina ran from one meeting to the next. Although she occasionally made to-do lists, she could never remember where she left them. She felt guilty because she had a reduced teaching load, but still could not seem to find any time to write. Not being an academic, Sabrina's partner could not understand why she was not able to get her work done during the 9 to 5 workday. All Sabrina's white junior colleagues were publishing prolifically and moving forward on externally funded projects, while she was slowly sinking. At the end of her second year, she had no publications, one article under review, and no written grant proposals. Sabrina was losing confidence and self-esteem by the day, but did not have anyone to confide in and did not know how anything could change.

While Sabrina may have understood the need for long-term planning at the abstract level, examining how she spent her time on a daily basis made it clear that she was operating on day-to-day crisis management. In many ways, she was the social science equivalent to Scott—both were surviving day to day, but making little progress toward the activities that would count most heavily in their promotion and tenure evaluations. Sabrina had let teaching take over her life and continued to operate on her undergraduate productivity cycle: (1) procrastinate, (2) stay up all night before the deadline, and (3) crash once the deadline was met. The lack of control she had over her daily work then impacted her psychological well-being. Sabrina told us, "I just can't get my shit together." Does this sound familiar? Is there anything in Sabrina's or Scott's story that reminds you of yourself?

Although it is important to have a five-year plan, clearly defined goals, and a list of projects and tasks that need to be completed each year on the tenure track, even the best plan is useless unless it is executed. We have found that one of the easiest and best tools for managing time is Julie Morgenstern's **time map**. Many of us keep appointment books and calendars, but a time map is different because it forces you to integrate your to-do list with your daily calendar. This means that you must commit time in your schedule to accomplish tasks. It is where your to-do list and your calendar merge into one useful tool.

Time mapping is particularly critical for academics because it is entirely possible that, in any given week, the only formal appointments you have are your classes and a few meetings. In between, there are large swaths of uncommitted time that can become consumed by activities unrelated to your long-term goals. You might be feeling at this point not only that five years is not a lot of time, but that there is an enormous number of things that need to be done in that short period. That apprehension is good because this, in fact, is the reality of life on the tenure track: too much to do and too little time to get it done.

Academic time mapping is based on the philosophy of *paying yourself first*. This means that the first things you mark out on your schedule each week are the things that are most important to your long-term goals (that means the work that gets taken care of first each day). If your goal is to win tenure at the community college where you have a heavy teaching load and no research expectations, then teaching preparation, office hours, and class time are first in your schedule. If you are trying to win tenure at a research-intensive university (like Scott, Brenda, and Sabrina), then research and writing time go first into your schedule. And if you are unhappy with your first job placement, and your goal is to be able to move to another institution, then the best thing you can do is to make research and writing your highest priority. Your research publications are your currency in the job market because they will keep you movable and marketable, and give you the only power you have as a tenure-track professor: the power to choose whether or not you want to stay at your current institution.

For Sabrina, we recommended that research and writing be the first things she did in the morning *before* checking e-mail, prepping for classes, and getting sucked into addressing everyone else's needs. Sabrina did this by blocking out her writing time in her calendar (as an appointment she had with herself). We then encouraged Sabrina to treat that commitment with the same respect she would give any other scheduled meeting: start on time, arrive prepared, and do not cancel it unless there is an emergency. This simple, yet powerfully symbolic, step of putting her writing time into her daily calendar each day for the entire semester sent a message to Sabrina's inner self and the universe that she was willing to align her time with her priorities. After Sabrina blocked out her writing and research time, she then added all the appointments and commitments she had with others (classes, faculty meetings, etc.) in her weekly calendar **for the entire semester**. Having set up the skeleton of her weekly schedule, Sabrina could begin to consider how her semester work plan could be accomplished on a week-by-week basis.

Once Sabrina had blocked out all the nonnegotiable time commitments in her schedule, she could then tackle her to-do list (composed of all the immediate tasks she needed to get done and the strategic tasks associated with the projects that would keep her on track with her five-year plan). With that information in hand, we recommended Sabrina set aside time each Sunday evening for a **Sunday meeting** to figure out what blocks of time she could actually assign to each task on her list. In other words, this was an hour to plan how to map her to-do list onto her calendar for the following week. Sabrina (like all faculty to whom we assign this unpleasant homework) had the same devastating realization *every single week*: she did not have enough time in her calendar to complete all the tasks on her to-do list. Each week, Sabrina was shocked by this realization, threw up her hands, gnashed her teeth, and occasionally cursed the very week itself for not having enough hours! But then she began to prioritize, delegate, lower her standards for nonessential tasks, compromise, and finally let go of the unnecessary items. Why did Sabrina put herself through this agony every week? Because she had learned that having more items on her to-do list than hours available was the reality of academic life. Even more important was facing the inevitable truth that it was far better for her to deal with that reality at the beginning of the week than to blindly come to that realization at the end of the week.

At the beginning of the week, Sabrina could make contingency plans by asking others for help, pushing back a deadline before she missed it, deciding she did not need to do something at all, or even giving herself permission to do something less than perfectly. It also became far easier to say no to additional requests when she fully understood how her time was being spent and that she did not have any to spare. Finally, Sabrina found time mapping worthwhile because she could make conscious decisions about how she spent her time. Instead of remaining in her old boom-and-bust cycle where she was frantically running to put out the next fire, Sabrina knew at the beginning of each week that everything important was going to get done, that she was making progress toward her long-term goals, and that she had the power to decide how her time would be spent.

Step 5: Create Accountability and Support

Even the most diligent, dedicated, and disciplined faculty members need **support** to execute their projects and tasks on a weekly basis. Although Chapter 10 is exclusively devoted to a discussion of how to create supportive social networks, we want to plant the seed here that you are not alone in working toward tenure and promotion. Neither are you alone in struggling to make time for your long-term goals in the midst of the chaos of your day-to-day schedule. But it is imperative that you proactively create local, virtual, or national support networks with others who are right there with you in the struggle. We find that the most effective support comes from accountability groups (described in Chapter 10) where faculty meet on a regular weekly basis in person, or online, in order to keep themselves writing and making regular progress on their long-term goals. These types of networks will help you to execute your plan every day and understand that everyone struggles with writing and time management. Sharing openly and honestly in that struggle helps us to better understand ourselves and our intellectual work, and works as a protective layer against the toxic environment of petty competition, egotism, and one-upsmanship that exists in many departments. One of our accountability group participants (an assistant professor in political science) described the process this way:

> My group helped me understand what keeps academics from writing. I now see that my challenges are not individual failings, but habits and responses that are widespread among faculty and often caused or exacerbated by the isolated conditions within which we work. The group provided me with a model for surmounting those challenges. Ultimately, this has enhanced my commitment to my department and the university. I'm interested in, and committed to, the success of my colleagues and the institution we work in to a degree I wasn't before.

Moving from a Reactive to Proactive Perspective

Of course, things do not always go according to plan and you have no way of knowing how the next five years will actually unfold. But, as author Barbara Sher writes, "Of all the forces that will be operating on your life over those 5 years—chance and love and loss and luck, health, and economics and history—*your wish and will*, your own unfolding, should be one of the strongest" (1979, p. 192). Brenda was clear and confident about her goal to transform her dissertation into a publishable book. She was the first person to admit that she had lots of work to complete, and that several factors in getting her manuscript published were out of her control. However, she also knew what was under her control (planning and execution) and had a clear sense of the projects and tasks that were necessary to make her goal a reality. The probability that her first book will actually get published is exponentially higher than for faculty like Scott who had great ideas, refused to plan, and irrationally expected that everything would simply fall into place based on the strength of their intellect and the habits that got them through graduate school.

We used Brenda's case study as an example to walk you through the **five steps of strategic planning for new faculty**: (1) identify your professional goals, (2) outline the projects and tasks that are necessary to achieve your goals, (3) map your projects onto time, (4) execute your plan on a daily basis, and (5) create accountability and support. It bears repeating that we only mapped one of Brenda's goals onto her five-year timeline. To complete her strategic plan, she must go through the same mapping process for all of her goals: publishing two articles from her dissertation research, winning a one-year fellowship or postdoc, designing her next book project, and getting promoted with tenure.

We regularly facilitate workshops in which we guide first-year faculty through the process of creating a five-year strategic plan. Without fail, their reactions to the idea of planning vary from outright refusal to giddy enthusiasm. For most faculty, planning their future is exciting because, once they write down the projects they will actually have to complete to make their goals a reality, they often feel a sense of clarity and control over their work. They are no longer subject to a hazy and mysterious process, but instead have a clear path. Their clarity about the magnitude of work they need to accomplish also creates a sense of empowerment to say no honestly and frequently to unnecessary service requests. They know that if they cannot fit something onto their time map, they do not have time to complete the request. For many, this level of clarity is liberating. That said, other faculty with whom we work go through the process of creating strategic plans but, when they see the amount of work ahead of them, they feel overwhelmed and frightened about the uncertainty of how successful a project will be, and question whether the amount of work required is worth the outcome. But all of these responses, questions, and self-reflections are only possible after having done the work to create a strategic plan. The strategic plan is then a living and breathing document, authored by you, and subject to your approval or amendment.

Perhaps the most important reason for planning your path toward tenure and promotion is that doing so moves you from a reactive position in your professional life to a proactive stance. Instead of scrambling to complete necessary tasks and projects at the last minute, planning and execution allow you to assert control over your work and your career. They spare you from the mental debilitation that arises when you find yourself trying to play catch-up, and give you an opportunity to influence your future mobility, which benefits you no matter what tenure verdict you ultimately receive. Certainly, if you employ a strategic plan and stick with it, you will greatly increase your chances of winning tenure, which is incredibly empowering. However, in the event that you dutifully develop and execute a strategic plan and are nonetheless denied tenure, you will benefit anyhow because you will have the clarity and comfort that come from knowing your denial was linked to factors other than your abilities, discipline, productivity, and accomplishments.

Knowing that you were diligent from the outset about defining and executing your goals, projects, and tasks provides a sense of resolve that you did all that was within your power, and any decision against you does not reflect on your worthiness, but rather some combination of sociopolitical factors were operating beyond your personal control. And of course, faculty who publish prolifically will have a much greater probability of success on the job market during their sixth year than those who have come to the end of the tenure track without much to show for it.

Because this book is about self-empowerment and about succeeding in spite of the odds against you, we cannot encourage you strongly enough to use the tools we offer here to forge a proactive rather than a reactive stance in your tenure pursuit. This is the best way to ensure that, whatever outcome you face, you can hold your head high knowing that you exercised mastery, power, and accomplishment over the one and only thing you had complete control over during your tenure-track years: yourself.

Takeaway Tips

- Create a five-year strategic plan by defining your professional goals, determining what projects are necessary to achieve your goals, and distributing those projects over years 1 through 5.

- Use time mapping to achieve your goals by dividing your annual goals into semesters, then mapping them onto a monthly calendar.
- Set aside one day a week for a Sunday meeting to plan the week by mapping your strategic and immediate to-do list tasks onto your weekly calendar.
- If you do not have a planner, close this book immediately and go buy one.
- Pay yourself first by blocking out writing time in your weekly calendar as an appointment for the entire semester, and do not compromise it.
- Learn to accurately assess how long it takes to complete tasks by keeping track of your time. Until then, guess how long it will take you and multiply that number by 2.5.

Suggested Readings

Boice, Robert. (2000). *Advice for New Faculty Members*. New York: Allyn and Bacon.

Morgenstern, Julie. (2004). *Time Management from the Inside Out: The Foolproof System for Taking Control of Your Schedule and Your Life* (2nd ed.). New York: Owl Books.

Sher, Barbara. (1979). *Wishcraft: How to Get What You Really Want*. New York: Ballantine Books.

Zerubavel, Eviatar. (1999). *The Clockwork Muse: A Practical Guide to Writing Theses, Dissertations, and Books*. Cambridge, MA: Harvard University Press.

5 | The Academic Office

Walk down the hallway in any academic department and you will see the full spectrum of office upkeep: chaos to order, darkness to light, filthy to immaculate, functional to stylish, homey to utilitarian, and near empty to bursting at the seams. Faculty members whose offices are at the extreme ends of the spectrum are well-known to colleagues, both for the order of their personal space (or lack thereof) and the organizational, behavioral, and professional traits associated with the state of their office. We believe that it is important to briefly consider the state of the academic office because your office sends a message—intended or not—about you to others. For example, a black full professor at a large urban research university was asked to join the dean's office as an associate dean. The professor agreed to discuss the matter if the dean would meet with him in his current campus office. Upon the dean's arrival, the professor swung open his office door to reveal a frightening level of chaos. With a single grand gesture, the professor said, "This is why I probably should never work in the dean's office." No further explanation or conversation was required. The dean silently turned on her heels and left. It is important to remember that the space in which you work can be a powerful tool for making an impression *and* it can significantly impact your productivity. To begin, there are three basic questions about physical space that we encourage junior faculty to consider:

1. What impression does your office convey about you to others?
2. Is this the impression you want to communicate?
3. Are you able to function efficiently in your work space(s)?

Impression Management

It is critical for all junior faculty to contemplate the impression that their office conveys, but it is especially important for black faculty. You may be wondering why deep-thinking intellectuals should care about something so superficial as an office. The reality is that all of us are prone to assessing other people's competence by evaluating their appearance and performance. Superficial but true, most perceived credibility comes from a person's physical appearance and the way that they speak, while precious little is determined by what they actually say. As a black faculty member, you are more visible than your white colleagues and, as a result, everything you do is more noticeable. Yes, this is unfair, but unfortunately it also is true, and that means you have to consider how you appear to others. At the same time, it also is important to realize that conscious management of the impression you give to others can be empowering. You can create a professional persona that will communicate specific messages to others and that will act as a protective layer around you. Developing a professional persona with clear boundaries can protect you from both students and colleagues who try to consume inappropriate amounts of time and from those who want you to do things that are not in your best interests.

Your physical appearance is made up of numerous components: clothing, physical traits, demeanor, stance, and language usage. But your office also plays a role in how you appear to others because it makes a statement about who you are as a professional. The order, cleanliness, furniture, lighting, and presence of personal items can encourage various types of behavior by cuing people about what is (and is not) acceptable in your space.

When Kerry Ann was in graduate school, one of the white male faculty members in her department was notorious for the disheveled state of his office. He kept such a large stack of papers on his desk that a student seated across from him was able to see only the professor's eyes and forehead. His bookshelves were packed with books and twisted, crinkled, wadded-up paper. Visitors could hear their shoes crushing snack food remnants as they perilously meandered around the books, papers, and miscellaneous items on his office floor. Despite the fact that this professor was the director of graduate studies, his untidiness discouraged both students and other faculty from visiting him. Students met with him only when they were experiencing dire emergencies, and returned to the graduate student lounge with stories about the rodents and the ever-increasing height of the paper pile on his desk. Yet, as repelled as people were by his office, the professor's behavior was strategic. Consciously or unconsciously, he had perfected the "mad genius" persona. However disgusting, everyone respects a mad genius—at least if he is white and male. The important point to this story is that black faculty can pull this off only if they have already demonstrated genius (like the example of the full professor at the beginning of this chapter). Otherwise, colleagues will be more likely to attribute office mess to negative stereotypes like "dirty," "unkempt," or "unprofessional."

One reason black faculty have to be especially mindful of managing the impression their office creates is that they are likely to be bombarded by visitors their white colleagues will never face. For example, it is a common (albeit unspoken) expectation that black faculty will serve as mentors to black students on campus. Black students will seek you out irrespective of whether (or not) they are students in your class, majors in your department, or have any interest in your research simply because you are a black faculty member. Generally speaking, white faculty do not face this experience unless they are underrepresented in some way (i.e., white women in the natural sciences or engineering). It would seem strange to many white male faculty if a random white student showed up at their office door expecting them to have time to listen to their concerns, understand their problems, and help them formulate solutions *just because they were white*. Although it is understandable that black students will choose to seek out black faculty members for mentoring and as important role models, this is one of many examples of additional people who will knock at your door besides your students and colleagues. And this is why you need to think clearly about whether your office space may excessively encourage people to drop by and linger.

Cynthia was a junior faculty member in the social sciences at a liberal arts college in the South where she taught four courses per semester. A petite woman in her late twenties, she wore jeans and a cotton T-shirt to campus on most days. Students at her college packed her classes every semester and her office hours were equally busy. Having just received her third year review, Cynthia was disappointed and frustrated that her contact with students went unrecognized while her lack of publications was the focal point of the mainly negative review. Although she was reappointed, her department made it clear that she would need to publish her book and several articles in order to win tenure. Cynthia was not sure how that could happen because of all the time she spent with her students. These interactions were fulfilling, but she also felt unable to turn away the black students and overwhelmed by the sheer number of students who came to her door.

Cynthia came to us to help her find some balance in her workday. We advised her to keep track of how she spent her time for two weeks so that we could see where all of her time was going. Like many faculty, she was spending the least amount of time on research (two hours per week), yet she was spending ten hours per week (about two hours per day) meeting with students in office hours, individual appointments, or student groups. This ten hours was in addition to her teaching and course preparation time (twenty-four hours per week). It was clear that Cynthia's overall appearance (her small stature and casual dress) sent the messages "young" and "approachable" to her students. Her demeanor was friendly and she often hugged students and warmly welcomed them to her office, which looked more like a comfortable and inviting living room than a work space. The office was immaculately clean, full of family photos, furnished with a gigantic couch and ottoman, and a hot pot of tea was perpetually brewing to be shared.

Cynthia could not understand why students came to her office in droves and never left, or why colleagues dropped by and lingered. She sometimes feigned an appointment elsewhere just to get them to leave. However, this was inefficient because she then had to leave her own office just to maintain the ruse. We gently encouraged Cynthia to step outside of herself in order to take a look at her office and a typical interaction that took place in it. She described an average interaction as follows:

> Someone knocks on my (always open) door. I hop up in an excited manner and answer with a big smile, warm southern greeting, and occasionally a hug. I stand off to the side in a way that says, "Come on in and set a spell. I'm not busy." Of course, the visitor enters my place of refuge, inhales the fresh potpourri, and melts into my big, fluffy floral couch for a lengthy conversation. I sit at the edge of my seat, making prolonged eye contact, head tilted inquisitively, and listening intently. As the conversation goes on, I readily offer chocolates from my candy dish or a tissue (as needed). The call continues until the visitor feels the interaction has concluded and decides to leave. Another hug is dispatched and anywhere from twenty minutes to an hour of my time is gone.

We then asked Cynthia to compare a typical visit to her office with an actual visit to her boy-wonder colleague next door, who rarely received guests even though he was a young junior faculty member like herself. The next time she heard a knock at her colleague's door, she went out in the hall to discreetly observe the interaction. Boy wonder opened the closed door a mere two feet and put his body in the doorway. His greeting was spoken with flat affect and intonation: "What?" The student was unfazed and simply stated her business while standing in the hallway. He gave the student a three-sentence response. She said "Thank you," and promptly left. Although Cynthia could not quite imagine herself responding to a student in the same way, she realized how different her behavior was from that of her white male colleague, how his brief response was unproblematic to the student, and why he had so much time to write. The lesson was clear: cracked door + body block + limited greeting = few and quick visits. The key for Cynthia was to understand that there are multiple possible responses to any given situation, and that she can consciously choose how to present herself at different times and with different people.

Considering Institutional Norms

As with every piece of advice you read in this book, the context for evaluating how to respond to internal and external factors is the set of norms at your particular institution. Both of us have worked in small private liberal arts colleges where the departmental norm was that faculty worked eight hours a day in their campus office. Monday through Friday, most of our colleagues trickled in between 8:00 and 10:00 A.M., there was a general buzz about the office throughout the day, and between 4:00 and 6:00 P.M. people packed up and went home. Any new faculty member who had the audacity to work from home was in trouble because these departments functioned like a fraternity house, with everyone acutely aware of each other's comings and goings, accompanied by an unending stream of speculation, wisecracks, gossip, and criticism. It was also abundantly clear from the outset that our senior colleagues were operating on the old-school equation that having one's butt in the office equals work, while having one's butt at home equals play. As a result, a faculty member's reputation as a hard worker was based almost entirely on whether or not he or she clocked in for an eight-hour day on campus. For each of us, this punch-the-clock mentality seemed restrictive and was inconsistent with our personal patterns of work and productivity. We both are far more productive working at home than we ever will be at the office with its constant interruptions. But it did not matter if we were sweating blood at home over a manuscript while another colleague was shopping on eBay in his office. The person who was physically in the office eight hours a day was considered a "hard worker" per the culture of our respective institutions. Those who worked at home, where people could only imagine them watching television and eating potato chips, were described as "never around" and were considered "lazy," "uncommitted," or "not team players." Therefore, junior faculty must figure out the norms and values of their department if they want to cultivate a positive first impression.

The point is that, during the first semester of any faculty appointment, you will have to make deliberate and strategic decisions about your work space if you want to make a positive first impression. Things will get easier after that, but it is incredibly difficult to overcome a negative first impression. Making a positive impression may require some uncomfortable adaptations to the prevailing department norms, but they are necessary. These adaptations likely will be temporary because, once people have it set in their mind what "kind" of colleague you are, they will tolerate greater flexibility in how and where you work. During Kerry Ann's first semester working at a small private liberal arts college, she adapted by getting up early and writing at home before driving to campus each day. She was then at campus within the accepted norms of the workday and could set up the last part of her afternoon (when she had zero energy) for tasks unrelated to work that could be completed quietly in her office. Because she was in a temporary office that was located directly in the center of departmental activity, everyone knew when she arrived and when she left. Writing at home in the early morning hours meant that she was able to get her most important work done on her own terms, while also satisfying the unstated department requirement for "hard workers" (physical presence on campus eight hours a day). After a semester, Kerry Ann moved to her permanent office, which was far removed from the main department (so much so that it was referred to as "death row"). But by then, her reputation as a diligent, hardworking team player was already solidified so that she could work at home more often with none of her colleagues even noticing.

Importantly, departments differ and, although an eight-hour day on campus was the norm when we worked at small liberal arts colleges, it was exactly the opposite when we were colleagues at a large, rural public university. The institution was situated in an isolated rural location, but it was within commuting distance from several different cities. As a result of this location, the majority of faculty lived in other cities (some in adjoining states), and they came to campus only on days when they taught classes. On most days, you could shoot a cannonball down the middle of the hallway without the slightest fear of hitting anyone. Attributions such as hardworking and team player were determined by a faculty member's quantity of publications and external grant funds. Spending too much time on campus was perceived as suspect because it took away from the ability to publish and secure grants. Here, a different context required different behavior to make a positive first impression. Because of the variation in institutional cultures, be cognizant of your institutional norms when making decisions about where you will work, what time of day you will work, how you will respond to visitors, and whether your office door will remain open or closed. If you want to make a positive first impression, adapt to the norms of your institution. If you are unable or unwilling to do so, then understand what the consequences of your choices will be.

Functional Efficiency

Even more important than considering the messages that your office conveys to others is having an office that enables you to be efficient in your research and teaching. Efficiency requires that you can find *what* you need *when* you need it, manage the flow of paperwork streaming in from every direction, and keep on hand what is necessary for writing up your research. Additionally, successful junior faculty members find ways to manage the amount of time spent on teaching. We discuss this in greater detail in Chapter 7, but the building blocks necessary to teach efficiently are a clear filing system, a simple paper management system, and a system for keeping track of tasks. Once your time and energy have been freed up from teaching, searching for things you cannot find, and trying to figure out what bureaucratic tasks you have or have not done, they can be devoted to your scholarship. Time and again, we have observed how faculty who organize their office space, create a calendar, and commit to daily writing increase their productivity. This daily movement forward allows them to make continuous progress on their research and therefore experience an increased sense of professional competence and reduced anxiety. And as an important by-product, their organized office projects the message to others that their research is under control and their agenda is moving forward.

Getting Your Space Organized

Interestingly, a lack of organized space is a concern for many academics. Kerry Ann's campus office is immaculately clean, modern, and organized. It features minimalist furnishings and is constructed for maximum efficiency. In this small space, Kerry Ann has room for herself, her graduate students, and her undergraduate assistants and their work materials. Because of its location on her department's floor, it is a highly visible space. If her door is open (which is frequent), the inside of her office is the first thing that people see when they exit the elevator. Her office is somewhat of a Rorschach test because it never fails to elicit comments from passersby and visitors, and the comments are typically revealing of the speakers' self-assessment and desires: "Oooohhh, it's so neat!" "You're sooooo organized." "Even *I* could be efficient in an office like this!" "I wish I could get organized." "I will never be organized, it's hopeless." "Can you come fix my office?"

Of course, we can't "fix" anyone else's office because what is functional for either of us most likely will not be functional for anyone else. As an academic and as a therapist, our daily activities differ significantly. As a result, the work that is done in our offices and the organization of our offices are also quite different. We want to be clear that "organized" means only that you can find what you are looking for when you need it. The actual appearance of that organization can vary dramatically from one faculty member to another, and we are not advocating that everyone's office should look like an advertisement from The Container Store. There is no single, cure-all system that works for everyone, much less all academics. Faculty members have different practical and psychological issues underlying their disorganization as well as great variation in what constitutes "work." In other words, even among faculty in the same institution, the work that we do and what it means to have efficient space differ greatly. The office spaces of poets, mechanical engineers, sociologists, mathematicians, and biomedical researchers will look and feel different from each other. What is critical is whether the space is efficient and the organizational system reflective of the individual faculty member.

The remainder of this chapter provides strategies for creating space that will allow you to function effectively in whatever type of research and teaching you perform. Too often faculty consider organizing to be a God-given gift. Like singing, they think it is bestowed in abundance on a lucky few while others totally lack it. Sometimes those who wish for organized space believe it is an impossible reality because the actual process of organizing is boring; a waste of time; and, even if they could withstand the process of "getting organized," the blissfully organized office would be impossible to maintain over time. At the same time, we frequently hear colleagues describe how their disorganization leaves them feeling overwhelmed, embarrassed, cramped, out of control, incompetent, and floundering. They want to stop wasting so much time looking for things, achieve more in less time so they can spend time on what is really important to them, reduce their stress and anxiety, gain control over their work, and feel better about themselves professionally. And yet, most of us do not know where to start because nobody ever taught us how to make our space work for us. We begin with the basics of organizing your office space and then move into the details of developing a filing system.

Designing an Office That Works for You

If you are happy with the current state of your office, then please feel free to skip the remainder of this chapter. If not, pause here to ask yourself two questions: (1) What IS working for me in this office space? and (2) What is NOT working for me in this office space? Organization guru Julie Morgenstern (2004) suggests that disorganized office space is caused by one of three types of problems: (1) technical errors, (2) external realities, or (3) psychological obstacles. What she calls "technical errors" are the easiest to resolve because they are entirely within your control. Technical errors occur because you do not have a designated place for items, you have a confusing system, or you have no system at all to organize your office. External realities are more difficult because they result from things that are out of your control, such as an unrealistic workload or the fact that you may be in a spatial transition (e.g., moving offices) or life transition (e.g., having a baby). The final obstacles are the psychological blocks to getting organized, which include, but are not limited to unclear goals and priorities, fear of success or fear of failure, fear that order will cause loss of creativity, dissatisfaction with the office space, and the need for perfection.

Do any of these problems sound familiar? We bring them to your attention because it is important not only to be aware of your discontent with the work space, but also to understand why it is not working for you. Knowing why will allow you to determine whether it is something that can be resolved by reorganization of your space or whether there are some deeper issues that you may want to explore further. We focus the remainder of our discussion on the technical errors that are most common for academics. We will save for Chapter 6 some of the psychological obstacles that can be exacerbated in the ultracompetitive world of academic institutions.

Corey was an assistant professor of sociology and African American studies at a small, private research-intensive university in a large urban area infamous for its traffic congestion. She was single and, in order to maximize her opportunities to meet friends and potential partners, she chose to live in an area of the city that was heavily populated with young professionals of color. She was able to find a comfortable old house with the one thing she longed for, but never had, in graduate school: a large study. Corey was a radical black intellectual and community activist who had never spent a single moment thinking about "organizing her office." But after her first year, she felt spread out and frustrated. She had a home office, two campus offices (one in the Sociology Department and another in the African American Studies Department), and a small carrel in the library. Within those offices, she had a total of three separate computers, four sets of bookshelves, three filing cabinets, and no idea where to find anything!

Corey had several typical organizational problems, including: (1) she never had what she needed when she needed it, (2) her commute was too long to allow for any errors, (3) she was simultaneously resistant to the idea of "getting organized" and frustrated by her disorganization, (4) she was overrun by paper and information, and (5) her files were everywhere. We assured Corey that very little time was necessary to set up a system to resolve her organizational problems and improve her overall productivity. It seemed clear to us that Corey had to figure out what activities she did in each work space and then move the necessary materials into that space, develop a filing system, and come up with a basic strategy for handling the deluge of paper and information we all face on a daily basis.

Step 1: Determine What Activities Need to Occur and Where They Will Get Done

The most effective way to start organizing your office space is first to ask yourself: what activities do I need to perform in this space? Corey's home office was her primary office, where she wrote, read, thought, analyzed data, and handled daily correspondence. She used her Sociology Department office primarily for teaching preparation, conducting office hours, and storage of teaching materials and service-related files. Her office in the African American Studies Department was almost entirely empty and she used it only for overflow storage and meeting with colleagues in that department. Her library carrel served as a remote location where she could escape to work in solitude for a few hours on days that she had meetings at the beginning and end of the workday. We encouraged Corey to make a list of the activities that constituted her "work," think seriously about the best location for each of those activities, and realistically reconsider the necessity of four different work spaces.

Step 2: Connect the Materials and the Location

Once you determine the activities that you will conduct in your office space, you can determine the materials and supplies you will need. Corey mapped out her work activities and separated them according to what she planned to do in each work space. Her analysis of location, activities, and necessary materials is summarized in Table 5.1. By completing this exercise, Corey realized that having multiple offices was neither necessary nor efficient. She decided to concentrate her work in two office spaces: her Sociology Department office and her home office. She gave up the library carrel after admitting that she had used it only twice in an entire year, and decided to wait one year to make a decision about the African American Studies Department office.

Table 5.1   Planning Space and Materials

Activity	Necessary Items	Location
Write	Computer, pens, notepads, printer	Home office
Read	Books, journals, newspapers, magazines, comfortable chair, warm throw	Home office
Think	Large butcher paper, markers, glitter pens, pink stilettos, snacks, coffee, CDs, large worktable, corkboard-covered walls	Home office
Handle daily correspondence	Phone, computer, recycling bin, shredder	Home office
Analyze data	Data, computer, printer, SPSS, HyperResearch, binders, highlighters, phone numbers of coauthors, phone	Home office
Hold office hours	Not-too-comfortable visitor chair	Campus office
Teaching preparation	Desk, chair, computer, teaching files, teaching props, student papers, various colored pens, in-box and out-box, class books and articles	Campus office
File storage	File cabinets, extra file folders, labels, labeler, "to be filed" box	Campus office
Meeting preparation	Service files, desk, chair	Campus office

After determining the activities you will engage in within your office(s) and identifying what supplies you will need, it is necessary to dedicate time to sorting through the space and moving specific materials to the location where that work will occur. This was the most time-consuming task for Corey because it required that she go through her different work spaces, figure out what materials were necessary in each, and move the remaining materials to their proper location.

Step 3: Arrange the Space for Maximum Efficiency

Once everything that you need is in the right place, we suggest using Julie Morgenstern's (2004) simple, but highly effective, technique: the kindergarten model organization. She argues that a kindergarten classroom is the most efficient space ever because it has the following characteristics:

- The room is divided into activity zones.
- It is easy to focus on one activity at a time.
- Items are stored at their point of use.
- It is fun to put things away because everything has a home.
- There is a visual menu of everything that is important.

Corey was skeptical about the kindergarten model and even found the idea to be annoying. But she agreed to try the model as she redesigned her spaces. She rearranged her campus office into separate zones for student meetings, file storage, teaching preparation, and meeting preparation. The student meeting space was composed of a small, uncomfortable chair (she did not want furniture that put students in a confessional mode, lest they stay too long). Because Corey's office was quite small, she swiveled her wheeled desk chair around to create a meeting space. The desk served as her teaching preparation area. The wheels on her chair also allowed her to swivel to the filing cabinet, allowing her to access necessary files. Corey's teaching materials and student papers were kept on shelves next to her desk. The desk was also Corey's service preparation area and provided everything she needed within her reach. Corey's home office was twice the size of her campus office so she could separate her work zones there in different parts of the room itself. She created separate zones for data analysis, writing, reading, thinking, and correspondence, each of which held all the tools that she needed within reach.

The final organizational tool that made it all work for Corey is what we call the Brunsma research queue (BRQ). Our colleague David

Brunsma claims that this visual flowchart of research and writing was "given to him in a dream." After making the BRQ physically manifest, he shared it with us and we have used it ever since with great success (see Figure 5.1). The system is simple and requires only a large bulletin board (the bigger the better as a visual signal to yourself about the importance of research to your daily work), tacks, and bulldog clips (they look like the clips at the top of a clipboard). Once the bulletin board is

Figure 5.1 The Brunsma Research Queue

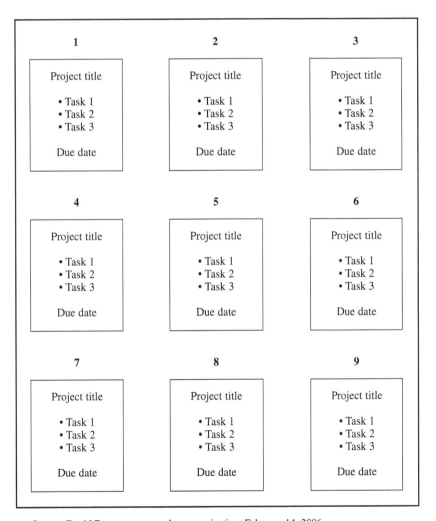

Source: David Brunsma, personal communication, February 14, 2006.

properly hung on the wall, nine numbers with corresponding tacks are placed on it. On each tack, all of the materials related to a specific research task are clipped together with a single bulldog clip. On the front of the clipped packet is a cover sheet outlining the tasks that need to be done and the due date in large bold print (these can be either external deadlines or, better yet, deadlines that have been internally set in accordance with your individual strategic plan). This literally forces you to move all of the paperwork related to a project into one place, to get it off your floor or desk, and to order the projects in a queue from most important to least important. The genius of the BRQ is that it organizes all of the materials you need in one place, it provides an enormous visual reminder of what needs to be done, and it forces you to physically prioritize projects and tasks. It also provides great satisfaction because, as you complete tasks, you get to move them off the queue (and directly into your filing system).

We describe the BRQ system in detail not to suggest that you run out and implement it exactly as described here. It is a suggestion to stimulate your imagination about how you can organize the flow of your specific work. Corey started out with a problem: too many tasks and deadlines to keep track of in her head and too much paper everywhere. Although Corey realized that she needed to address the deeper issues of saying yes too often, getting overcommitted, and being more selective about her work so as to align her intellectual activities with her long-term goals and values, her immediate requirement was to figure out what had to be done, get the paperwork into one place, and order the flow of activity. As a result of being tired of these problems, she tried the BRQ as a system to resolve her problems and meet her needs. Like Corey, we encourage you to identify the problems that are holding you back in order to develop a system that can resolve them.

Step 4: Create Simple Rules for Handling Paper

In addition to the BRQ, Corey needed to address the persistent challenge to the harmony of her space: the never-ending influx of paper. We recommended that she work toward managing paper by using four simple guidelines. First, pick up department mail only one time per week (unless she was expecting something urgent). Because Corey had both home and campus offices, she needed to be sure that mail related to activities she performed at her home office was mailed to her there, while items that were directly related to work she performed on campus went to her campus mailbox. Second, we suggested that she sort her mail while standing over the recycling bin so that each piece of paper could either be immediately recycled or put in an "action box." Third, we asked her to mark any paper going into her action box with a brief Post-it note indicating what action needed to be taken ("fill out form and return," "decide whether to renew and return," "check calendar to see if I can attend," etc.). Finally, we asked Corey to set aside fifteen minutes at the end of each day to clean up her office. During this time, any paperwork that had accumulated and required action was added to her action box. Then, once a week, Corey brought the action box to her Sunday meeting so that she could block out time in her calendar to complete the tasks, delegate them, or let them go.

Filing Systems

Even though filing systems are critical to the functionality of an office space, most academics figure out their system by trial and error over a period of years. Many high-minded intellectuals believe it is a waste of time to think about how to organize a filing system. When we proposed that Corey spend time developing a filing system, she looked at us as if we had suggested she try a colonic. After rolling her eyes, she said, "People are dying and you want me to spend time designing a filing system?" We asked her how many hours she had wasted looking for paper and having to re-create documents that she had already written but could not locate. In the end, Corey decided that she would much rather use her valuable time and energy on the things that really mattered to her instead of searching for paper. To that end, we helped her create an efficient filing system that was:

1. Organized around the categories of her job responsibilities.
2. Simple and straightforward.
3. Based on the quick retrieval of items.
4. Synchronized with her hard drive.
5. Composed only of items she truly needed to retain.
6. Low maintenance.

If you can bear to continue reading about filing systems, we will expand on each of these six principles using Corey's system as an example. As with all examples in this chapter, please note that these are intended to provide you with an illustration of basic principles and not as a directive one-size-fits-all solution.

Principle 1: Organize Around the Categories of Your Job Responsibilities

Corey learned somewhere along the line that filing meant putting things in an A through Z format. As a result, her first filing system had tabs for A–Z, and everything that she thought worthy of filing was forced into a letter. As you can imagine, she could never find anything because it was not clear whether her fabulous lecture "The Research Process" was filed under L for lecture, R for research, or T for teaching. After the 100th time of losing the lecture notes she needed for class *that* day, Corey was willing to admit her system was not working. We suggested that she separate her teaching files from everything else. At a minimum, that would reduce the number of file folders she had to rummage through to find the brilliant lecture "The Research Process."

An efficient filing system should reflect three to five main job responsibilities. For most academics these are: (1) research, (2) teaching, and (3) service. Ideally, you will need two four-drawer vertical filing cabinets. You can divide these drawers up in any way that matches your specific needs, but we recommend dividing them by priority. For example, if you are divided 40-30-30 among research-teaching-service, then let your file space reflect that distribution so that four drawers are allocated to research, two drawers to service, and two drawers to teaching. It also is helpful to assign a color to each of the separate areas and to use file folders only in those colors. For example, all research folders could be red, all teaching folders blue, and all service folders yellow. Not only will this make you look organized to the casual bystander, but you can glance at the files on your desk and know what they are (in general) without having to look at the specific titles. This color coding and categorical filing also makes it very easy to explain to an assistant how to file for you, or to a graduate student who may need to access files in your office when you are not there. When thinking about what to actually file under research, teaching, and service, try to keep Principle 2 in mind.

Principle 2: Simple and Straightforward

The point of this guideline is to avoid the greatest error that faculty make in creating a filing system. We are complicated creatures who seek complexity in most things. As a result, we tend to create hundreds of files, each containing one or two pieces of paper. This error occurs because we do not think of our files as reflecting our activity. For example, at one point, Corey kept a separate file for each of the courses she taught. Given that she taught at least ten different courses, and that there was overlap in the content of these courses, she had a big mess (lots of duplicate items and no clarity as to the courses they were filed under). We suggested to Corey that it would be much more efficient to create one large teaching category. In this large category, she organized subcategories as the subfields of her discipline that she introduced to students in her Introduction to Sociology course. The remainder of the classes that Corey taught were specific to one of these disciplinary subfields. That meant the subsections that she teaches as stand-alone classes were larger than those that she only touched on in the Introduction to Sociology course. For example, Corey had lots of files in the family category because she taught a course entitled "Marriage and Family" each year, and few in the deviance category because it was only a topic she discussed in her "Intro" course. But whenever she taught any course, she could work out of the same filing cabinet so there were no duplicate files and thus no confusion. When the opportunity came to design a new seminar on a specialized topic, Corey was able to quickly pull together the core elements that she covered in every class (what is sociology, social theory, and the research process) together with specialized elements that she would use in only that seminar. And as she developed new courses, her filing system simply expanded in size to accommodate that particular subfield, without fundamentally changing the structure of the system.

Principle 3: Quick Retrieval of Items

When setting up a system, think about how you will look for an item, not how you think it should be rationally stored. Emphasizing retrieval means that, when thinking about where Corey should file a document, we asked her, "Where will you look for it?" The secret to successful retrieval is having the fewest possible places to look for an item. For example, when Corey filed her lecture "The Research Process," she placed it in a blue folder (blue = teaching). Then, she placed it under a tab for research methods in which all the materials pertaining to the teaching of research methods were filed. She labeled the specific file "Lecture—The Research Process."

Once Corey began to experience the benefits of her filing system, we encouraged her to take the final plunge: create a file index that listed all of her file categories and subcategories. She posted this near her files and kept a copy in her briefcase with some Post-it notes. As she accumulated papers while away from her campus office, she scanned her index and stuck a Post-it note on the paper indicating where it should be filed. When she returned to her office, filing those newly acquired papers was a quick and effortless chore for her (or, better yet, for her undergraduate assistant).

Principle 4: Synchronize Your Paper Files and Your Hard Drive

This principle should be simple and obvious, but many people get stuck here. The goal is to have harmony between your hard drive and your paper files. Therefore, on your hard drive, create the same categories that you use in your paper filing system. For example, Corey had three folders on her hard drive: (1) research, (2) teaching, and (3) service. In this way, the electronic files on her hard drive had the same foundational logic as everything in her file cabinet.

Given that paper files and electronic files need to be synchronized, it is equally important to synchronize the computers that you work on. One of the most frequent complaints we hear is that faculty members do not know what files are on what hard drive. There are many possible solutions, but the simplest seems to be one of the following: (1) work primarily on one (and only one) computer that is automatically backed up on your college's server, (2) purchase software that allows you to synchronize your home and office computers, or (3) set up an independent Web-based system for your files so that you can access them no matter where you are. Corey chose the third option and used a free Yahoo! group to keep her electronic files. She preferred this option because she worked with a number of students who required access to her electronic files and they could locate them in this private, Web-based environment at their convenience.

Principle 5: Keep Only Items That You Truly Need to Retain

According to Julie Morgenstern (2004), 80 percent of what gets filed is never referred to again. Many of us believe that we need to keep every piece of paper that comes across our desk just in case we might need it in the future. We recommend becoming more selective about what you choose to put into your file cabinet in the first place. In short, it is crucial to learn to determine what is "core information" and what is momentarily fascinating, but unnecessary.

That said, all filing systems need some maintenance: pruning, expanding, and contracting as needed. Take one afternoon on each of your semester breaks (summer vacation, winter break, and spring break) to go through your filing cabinet, make room for expansion in areas where it is necessary, and toss things out that are no longer required, such as duplicate copies of documents, previous drafts of writing, and articles that you do not want to read again. Generally speaking, if you have not accessed something in a year, you are not going to use it or it is out of date (with the exception of articles you consider to be "classics"). Reassess your categories, update your file index, and make new labels for anything that needs them. This takes little time, but it will remind you of what is in your files and help you to maintain efficiency.

Principle 6: Minimal Maintenance

A well-designed system requires minimal upkeep. You will be in and out of your files on a daily basis because they are a critical part of your work and a communal resource for your students (who also can be in and out of them daily). When you file, quickly scan and clean out unnecessary papers. Also, remain open to the creation of new files. Keep a supply of colored folders and a label maker on hand for this purpose. As you create a new file, you can either write a label in pencil and add it to the system later, or you can take thirty seconds to make a professional-looking label for it.

The reason Corey enjoyed her new filing system so much is that she finally knew where everything was. More importantly, the system saved her time and mental energy for things that she really wanted to do (of which filing was not high on the list). It allowed Corey to come to her campus office before class, pull out her lesson plan and lecture notes to review them, and then place them back in the filing cabinet immediately after returning from class. And if she was in a rush, she could ask her teaching assistant to access the file and meet her at the lecture hall. For a meeting, Corey needed to pick up only a file from the yellow service area, review it briefly, and head to the meeting. By taking the time to organize, Corey stopped wasting energy trying to figure out where things were. Your files may be out in the open, they may be piles and not files, and they may look like a junk heap to those who do not understand your system. But that is okay as long as you know where to find things when you need them, you feel good about your space, and you can work efficiently in it. Having an office space that works well for you feels great and is well worth the time it takes to get there!

Takeaway Tips

- Your office is one factor in how you appear to others as a professional. Figure out what impression you want it to convey and arrange your office accordingly.

- Institutional norms vary as to where faculty work, so observe how much time other faculty spend in their offices, and whether or not doors are open or closed. Know what the norms are at your institution and set your working patterns within them if you want to make a positive first impression.
- An organized office decreases time spent on teaching and increases research productivity.
- Make sure that mail is sent to the right office and sort it over the recycling bin.
- Consider Morgenstern's kindergarten model of organization for your work space.
- Efficient filing systems are simply and straightforwardly organized around the categories of your job responsibilities, based on the quick retrieval of items, based on the same logic as your hard drive, and composed only of items you truly need to retain, and they require minimal maintenance.

Suggested Readings

Morgenstern, Julie. (2004). *Organizing from the Inside Out: The Foolproof System for Organizing Your Home, Your Office, and Your Life.* New York: Owl Books.
Morgenstern, Julie. (2005). *Never Check E-mail in the Morning: And Other Unexpected Strategies for Making Your Work Life Work.* New York: Fireside.

6 | Healthy Pathways to Publication

THOUGH it is conventional wisdom in academe that faculty must either publish or perish, there is precious little discussion about either the process of academic writing or the development of healthy pathways to **publication**. By this, we do not mean the highly discipline-specific steps that move research findings to publication, but rather the process of developing a regular writing routine that leads to the consistent publication of research to whatever degree your specific institution deems the "standard" for promotion and tenure. Certainly, institutions vary in their publication expectations and standards, and it is important for you to be clear as to what they are at your college or university. But once you understand the parameters of what you need to produce, the question becomes: how do you move toward that goal in a way that allows for you to do the intellectual work that you became an academic to do, while also meeting the high bar for publication set before you? In short, how do you *publish and flourish*?

As with every chapter in this section, we believe there are general challenges that all junior faculty face in making the transition from graduate student to professor as well as specific challenges that are unique to black faculty. Given that your job as a professor is the production and dissemination of knowledge (via research and teaching), the challenge to transitioning into your first academic position is to place your **research** and **writing** at the center of your daily activities. That is because research and writing are often simultaneously the highest priority (in terms of promotion and tenure) and the lowest priority (in terms of hours per week of time invested) for the typical new faculty member. Because black faculty receive disproportionately high service requests and demands on time, you will have to be particularly clear, aggressive, and proactive in carving out time for your writing.

Publishing is central to your professional success as an academic and as a black intellectual. It is also central to your ability to have the choice to move from your current institution if you are unhappy, or if you fail to receive a positive tenure decision. In terms of emotional health and personal well-being, it is vital that you redefine your relationship with writing and adopt practices that will enhance your productivity, lower your anxiety, and enable you to have a life outside of your institution. As a result, we first suggest that daily writing should serve as the foundation for developing a healthy and productive writing routine. We follow this with a discussion about the most common technical errors and psychological blocks that hold back many junior faculty from completing writing projects and publishing their work. We end with a broad array of suggestions to address whatever may be blocking you from realizing your own explosive creativity, productivity, and prolific publication record.

The Case for Daily Writing

For many new faculty members, the pressure to produce publications can make the writing process tedious, painful, and incredibly stressful. Rather than finding joy in the creative aspects of writing and the expansion of your research, it can feel like a heavy burden hanging over you twenty-four hours a day, seven days a week. Considerable research has been done on faculty productivity and the behavior patterns of prolific writers. For the vast majority of productive faculty, short daily sessions of writing result in completed manuscripts. Conversely, faculty who wait for large blocks of free time to enter into multiday writing binges often end up missing deadlines, worrying about their work, and waiting for those large blocks of time that just never quite emerge for a new assistant professor. Robert Boice (1989), one of the leading researchers in the area of faculty development, has conducted numerous studies of faculty writing and productivity. His findings are quite clear: scholars who write every day publish far more than those who write in large blocks of time. To make it concrete, if you want to be one of those new faculty who publish prolifically, the best way to do it is to set aside thirty to sixty minutes each day, Monday through Friday, exclusively for writing.

Do you still need more convincing? Boice conducted experimental research where he measured writing productivity among new faculty.

He followed three groups of junior faculty who attended one of his writing workshops for a year to determine how many pages they actually produced. The participants were divided into one of three groups. Group 1 did not change their writing behavior (i.e., they continued to wait for large blocks of time to write). Group 2 wrote every day and recorded their progress. Group 3 wrote every day, recorded their progress, and held themselves accountable to someone on a weekly basis. After one year, Boice (1989) calculated the average number of pages produced by each of the three groups. As you can see from the results in Table 6.1, Group 1's boom-and-bust cycle of writing resulted in an average of only seventeen pages produced. Group 2's simple act of writing every day and recording their progress increased the average number of pages produced to sixty-four. Most impressively, and central to our argument throughout this chapter, is that Group 3—those who added weekly accountability to daily writing and recording—produced 157 pages on average. Ask yourself: in which group do you want to be at this time next year?

For many academics, the undergraduate boom-and-bust cycle continues to be our unconscious default behavior pattern. As undergraduates, we procrastinated until the last minute, experienced anxiety and guilt, and then put everything in our life on hold for a few days before a deadline to crank out a twenty-page paper. For reasons that are not quite clear, faculty in many programs accepted our extremely rough drafts as completed work and dispensed perfunctory As. And we breathed a sigh of relief that we survived another semester. The problem is that, as we progressed to graduate school, our projects became larger, the days of last-minute writing frenzy stretched out to weeklong writing binges, and (because we were getting older) the post–writing-frenzy crash required a

Table 6.1   Boice's Experiment on Faculty Writing

Participating Groups	Average Number of Pages Written After One Year
Group 1: No change in writing behavior after boom-and-bust cycle	17
Group 2: Engaged in daily writing and recorded writing output	64
Group 3: Engaged in daily writing, recorded writing output, and were accountable on a weekly basis	157

Source: Robert Boice, "Procrastination, Busyness, and Bingeing," *Behaviour Research Therapy* 27: 605–611.

longer period of recovery time and was more costly to our physical health and relationships. Toward the end of graduate school, many long for a life free from the daily anxiety and guilt induced by procrastinating on our dissertations and imagine living in a state of confidence that projects will be completed by their deadlines without our relationships, homes, and physical health being turned upside down in the process. Unfortunately, precious few graduate students learn the simple key to make that possible: write for one hour a day.

We are most often contacted by junior faculty after they receive a critical third year review, when it has finally sunk in that their extraordinary levels of service are not going to overcome a lack of publications. They have been clinging to the boom-and-bust cycle; they are wedded to the idea that deep, serious academic writing can only be done in large blocks of time; and they are frustrated, miserable, and even angry about their lack of productivity. Yet despite the empirical fact that their current writing routine is not working, the faculty with whom we work tend to respond in one of two ways to our suggestion that they write for an hour a day: (1) they accept the idea enthusiastically, but fail to execute it; or (2) they deeply resist the mere idea of daily writing.

On the one hand, many black faculty we work with find the idea of daily writing attractive and reasonable, but cannot actually do it. They understand the concept and imagine how it might change their relationship to writing. But they just cannot make themselves write for one hour per day because they are too busy doing all the things in their professional life that are low priority, institutionally unsupported, and externally unrewarded. They spend dozens of hours preparing for their courses, doing in-depth grading, attending committee meetings, advising student groups, and various other invisible labor. Then, they hope to have energy at the end of the day to write. Of course, that end-of-the-day writing energy rarely appears so they continue in the cycle of promising that when _____ occurs (fill in with the summer vacation, winter break, or spring break), they will devote themselves to writing and make progress on their research. Regrettably, hoping to write at the end of the day does not work because it represents mental neglect of the one factor that is going to provide you with power and mobility in the academic universe: publications.

On the other hand, the resistance and reactivity to the mere idea of daily writing that we receive from faculty ("It just won't work for me.") is typically justified by some combination of false assumptions or fears. Resistant faculty tell us things such as: "My ideas are too big to even consider in thirty minutes a day." "I have a muse and can only write when he or she visits me." "Creativity is stifled by discipline." "I don't have thirty minutes a day to write; I have _____ [insert children, a medical practice, a heavy teaching load, etc.]." There is no amount of reasoning or documentation about the effectiveness of daily writing that will overcome their resistance. So, if you are reading this chapter and feeling resistant to the idea of daily writing, ask yourself where that resistance is coming from. What assumptions are you holding on to that lead you to assume that it will not work for you? Are you willing to move beyond your resistance, try it for thirty days, and then reevaluate?

Faculty who try daily writing report numerous unexpected benefits. As the pages pile up day after day, they feel a sense of forward motion on their research agenda. This increases their confidence and facilitates the transition from their role as graduate student to their new role as professor. Because daily writing has a generative quality, new ideas for future projects are constantly emerging. Incredibly, the faculty we work with often do not know what to do with all of the new ideas they come up with while writing each day. (We suggest jotting them down as they emerge and keeping them in a box or file labeled "my great new ideas" to be accessed at a later date.) When perpetual procrastinators try daily writing, they report experiencing a euphoric state after completing each day's entry. Knowing that they have done the hard work for the day, they can move forward, released from guilt and anxiety. They are free from ever having to stay up all night to rush a project through to completion at the eleventh hour. Instead, their daily writing enables them to have a regular sleep schedule, lower stress, and better overall physical health.

When it comes to encouraging new faculty to engage in daily writing, we may sound positively evangelical. But our zeal comes from having experienced firsthand the benefits of this simple strategy. Not only has it transformed our own curricula vitae (CVs) (by enabling us to complete a combined total of four books, twenty-four referred journal articles, and twelve chapters in edited volumes), but we have seen faculty we mentor, colleagues, graduate students, workshop participants, and coaching clients transformed by a simple, but firm, commitment to writing one hour per day.

We realize that this is easier said than done, that it requires a tremendous shift in your relationship to writing, and that you will need tremendous support in making the transition. We also understand that you may be facing a number of obstacles that preclude the possibility of daily writing at this moment and require some serious internal work to remove. We devote the remainder of this chapter to precisely those issues in the hope that, when you are finished reading, you will be willing and able to at least try daily writing for thirty days and see how it works for you.

What Is Holding You Back?

The first step in developing a healthy writing routine is to figure out why you do not currently have one. However, if you do, congratulations! You can go ahead and move on to the next chapter. But for the rest of us, it is worth taking the time to ask: what is holding me back? Through working with individual faculty and facilitating numerous writing groups, we have observed that there are many potential blocks to daily writing. A block may be caused by some combination of common technical errors and psychological obstacles. Of course, the answer to what is holding you back is something that only you can answer. But we hope this discussion of the most common blocks we have seen among junior faculty will help you to identify your own and develop some strategies for overcoming them as you move toward the development of a consistent and sustainable writing routine.

Technical Errors

Technical errors occur when you are missing some relevant skill or technique. For new faculty members, the skills and techniques that are necessary to develop a healthy writing routine are not typically taught in graduate school. Therefore, we see several consistent technical errors painfully repeated, such as

1. You have not set aside a specific time for your research and writing.
2. You have set aside the wrong time to write.
3. You have no idea how much time a particular research or writing task will take or you consistently underestimate the time a task will take.
4. You are the wrong person for the job (you think you have to do it all and that asking for help is a sign of weakness).
5. The tasks you have set out are too complex (e.g., items like "finish my book" are on your to-do list).
6. You cannot remember what you have to do because you do not believe in lists or calendars.
7. Your space is disorganized so you can never find what you need when you need it.

Most technical errors are easily surmountable by employing a small number of intentional techniques. Below we describe four simple techniques: (1) acquire a calendar, (2) schedule daily writing, (3) track your writing time, and (4) establish the Sunday meeting. Depending on which technical error(s) you are making, any one (or a combination) of these simple techniques can help you to start and maintain your daily writing habit.

Technique 1: Acquire a calendar. We do not want to belabor this point, but we have met far too many junior faculty who do not currently own a calendar or planner and seem to believe that they can retain all of their meetings, classes, commitments, and to-do items in their head. If you do not have a calendar, go buy or make one on your computer. It does not matter if it is an electronic system or a paper planner (often the simpler the system the more likely you are to use it consistently). What does matter is that you have a single way to block out the time you have available for writing and track your writing time.

Technique 2: Schedule daily writing. Block out between thirty and sixty minutes each day for writing. It is critically important that you put this time on your calendar as a first step toward aligning your time with your long-term goals. Many new faculty know that writing and publication are high priorities, but then behave as if writing is their lowest priority. In other words, despite knowing that writing is critical to professional success, these faculty relegate it to an optional daily activity. They "try to make time for it" at the end of the day, or "hope to get to it" after everything else has been done and everyone else's needs have been met. Ultimately, developing a healthy writing routine requires a fundamental reconceptualization of writing time by giving it the same weight in your schedule that it will have in your tenure review.

The challenge for everyone in making the transition from graduate student to professor is aligning your daily activity with your long-term goals and the criteria by which you will be reviewed. That means blocking out thirty to sixty minutes of each day for writing the same way that you would for a meeting or a class. Then, treat that writing time with the same respect and professionalism that you would your colleagues or your students. That means it is nonnegotiable; nothing else can happen during that time and, if anybody asks, the answer is "Sorry, but I'm not available at that time. I have a meeting." When you have completed your writing for the day, you can be absolutely certain that the most important aspect of your work is moving forward.

Technique 3: Track your writing time. Although unpleasant, it is incredibly useful to keep track of your writing time. Most of us have no idea how long writing tasks will take us to complete. As a result, we underestimate the time various tasks will require, and this can lead to an ongoing sense that we "aren't moving fast enough" or that we "take too long to get things done." This can result in unnecessary feelings of disappointment and frustration when, in fact, we are taking a reasonable amount of time. Instead of measuring yourself against an imaginary standard, it is far better to gauge yourself against your own behavior as a valid measurement standard. Tracking how long it takes to complete various tasks helps us not only to document our progress, but also to develop realistic expectations about how much work can actually get done in a particular period of time. This can then help us to plan realistically for our semester, our breaks, and our postdoc or fellowship years.

Technique 4: Establish the Sunday meeting. The Sunday meeting was previously mentioned in Chapter 4. It bears repeating because it is such a useful technique to overcome a multitude of technical errors. Try setting aside one hour at the beginning of each week to use as your weekly planning period. For the Sunday meeting, you will need your (1) strategic plan, (2) to-do list, (3) action box (if you have one), and (4) calendar. In that hour, try using the agenda items below.

1. Block your time commitments out of your weekly calendar. The meeting starts by marking out on the calendar your research and writing time, classes, office hours, and meetings. If you have not tried it yet, you may want to schedule your research and writing time first thing in the morning (before checking e-mail, preparing for classes, and responding to everyone else's needs in your workplace).
2. Create your to-do list. Write out all of your to-do items for the week, including the short-term tasks you need to get done, and the strategic tasks associated with your long-term research agenda. Some faculty like to categorize their to-do items under the headings "teaching," "service," and "research" to make sure that there is an appropriate balance and that they are not attending only to the immediate demands of teaching and service.
3. Map your tasks onto your time. Here is where it gets ugly! Turn back to your calendar for this week and assign each of your to-do items to a specific block of time. Inevitably, you will not have enough time in your calendar to complete all the tasks on your to-do list. Breathe deeply, knowing that this is normal, common, and the reality of academic life. No matter how frustrating it is, it is far better to deal with that reality at the beginning of the week than to walk blindly into that realization at the end of the week.

4. Proactively make decisions. Knowing that you have more tasks than time, consciously decide how you will spend your time during the week. You can break tasks that are too complex into smaller manageable tasks. You can delegate to others when you are the wrong person for the job. You can lower your standards for noncritical tasks. And you can decide that some tasks simply do not need to be completed and eliminate them from your list.

5. Commit to executing your plan. Of course, the best-laid plans can be thrown into disarray by unexpected circumstances. But having a clear plan and sincerely committing to its execution are essential to moving forward each week.

Psychological Obstacles

Unlike technical errors that can be addressed easily by making a behavioral adjustment or learning a particular skill or technique, psychological obstacles are far more difficult to address. This is partly because we rarely want to acknowledge that such blocks exist and partly because their roots can extend far back into our personal histories. We want you to at least consider the most common psychological blocks that we observe and, if they sound familiar, we encourage you to consider the ways that the faculty with whom we work have overcome them. The psychological obstacles most common to new faculty are (1) perfectionism, (2) disempowerment around writing, (3) unrealistically high expectations, and (4) unclear goals.

Academic perfectionism. Perfectionism is pervasive in academe and can manifest in a myriad of toxic ways. Most often, it just keeps us from writing (or finishing projects) because nothing is ever good enough. In its most paralyzing form, we cannot even put a word to paper because we have already judged it as garbage before it can hit the page! Perfectionism can emerge as a reaction to our fears: fear of humiliation, fear of criticism, fear that we will be discovered as an impostor, or fear of harsh judgment. Unfortunately, the structure of academe can be incredibly difficult for those with a perfectionist streak because, whenever we publish or present our work, it is guaranteed to be vigorously criticized, judged, and critically engaged. In a healthy environment, this can be invigorating. But more often, colleagues exaggerate any minor error, pounce on the slightest flaw in logic, and make both personal and substantive attacks for the purpose of their own ego aggrandizement. For scholars of color—particularly those who write about race or racism—

perfectionism can stem from believing that our work has to be utterly perfect and beyond reproach because of the extra scrutiny that we regularly encounter.

Strategy: tame your inner critic. In one of our writing groups, we asked participants to record their writing progress each day and describe their negative self-talk. Some initially refused, but others took great delight in recording the deluge of negative self-talk they faced while writing each day. It often was vicious, self-critical, angry, judgmental, and downright racist. Over the course of several weeks, participants found that it was a profound experience to consciously become aware of their inner critic's nonstop negativity. Recording the content of it each day, and reflecting on the patterns within that content, helped this group of junior faculty realize why they disliked writing so much. Who wants to face an angry inner critic on a daily basis?

Before we tried this exercise, the black faculty in our group were all fully aware that they live in a world where their presence and ideas are routinely devalued, dismissed, and openly disrespected. We had discussed this in the group on many occasions. But they had always imagined that those voices were "out there" and had not penetrated their interior world. Yet every week when we met and group members shared their inner critic's dialogue, they became increasingly aware of how deeply they had internalized the negative messages around them about not being good enough, not being smart enough, and not belonging in the academy. The outcome of unconsciously reproducing these messages in their minds had been diminished productivity. These faculty not only recognized their inner critic, but came up with images of how that critic was embodied (anyone from a popular movie villain to a specific person in their life). Once they could visualize their inner critic and become familiar with his or her demeaning dialogue, they were able to tell the critic to take a hike when he or she got out of hand at their writing desk.

The first step toward taming your inner critic is to write consistently every day and take note of the kind of mental messages that emerge while you are writing. At the end of your writing time, record your progress, your negative self-talk, and what you are proud of accomplishing that day. If it is helpful to you, go ahead and imagine what your inner critic would physically look like. At the end of the week, take a few minutes to look at the daily log of your negative self-talk to see what patterns exist. Once you see the patterns, gently ask yourself where those messages came from. Are they the words of a judgmental parent, childhood teacher, or graduate school faculty member? Are they true or are they falsehoods? Is it fair criticism of the work you are doing at that moment or merely old tapes of negativity that keep playing over and over again? Once you can visualize your inner critic and clearly recognize the common themes in that criticism, start working to imagine alternative and supportive messages to replace your critic's negative self-talk whenever it emerges.

Disempowerment around writing. When we ask faculty to describe their writing process, some describe it as one where they must be "inspired" before writing or unexpectedly "touched by a muse," at which time they drop everything and sink into a multiday writing frenzy. Although we hear this often, we still are stunned that otherwise rational people who are on a rapidly ticking tenure clock feel comfortable waiting to be touched by the muse in order to fulfill the primary requirements of their job: **research**, **writing**, and **publication**. The reason that many new faculty are put in danger by waiting for inspiration is that this strategy actually worked for them during graduate school when they had fewer commitments. Unfortunately, waiting on the muse works for few people after the transition to faculty because of the exponentially greater responsibilities, pressures, and demands on their time.

Strategy: control your writing. It seems that some faculty cling to the myth of the muse because they conceptualize writing as an externally driven process that is beyond their individual control. When we hear new faculty say that they write only when they are inspired to do so, it signals to us that they have not yet internalized the fact that writing is an integral part of their job. We do not wait to be inspired to teach our classes or to be touched by the "meeting muse" before attending a committee meeting—we just do these things as normal everyday activities. Writing is no different.

If you feel that you have to wait for an externally generated impulse to write, try critically engaging your core assumptions about the writing process and considering the idea that you control your writing. Academic writing does not just happen in a fit of artistic inspiration. Instead, articles and books are completed only when great ideas meet hard work over sustained periods of time. And as any daily writer knows, inspiration and creativity burst forth while you are actually writing. All you have to do is show up at the designated time and get started because the flow of ideas is catalyzed by the physical act of writing. If you are currently operating under the myth of the muse, that is perfectly fine. If it works for you and you are publishing prolifically, that is great. But if you are writing only when you feel inspired and you are not as productive as you need to be, then we encourage you to gently and lovingly ask your-self the following questions: Is this working for me? Where did this idea come from? Is it effective in the current stage of my career? Am I likely to meet the expectations for publication at my institution by relying on the muse? What will it take for me to consider writing as an everyday activity (just like grading papers or attending a faculty meeting)?

Unrealistically high expectations. One block to writing that emerges frequently among black faculty on the BlackAcademic.com discussion forum, in writing groups, and in individual sessions is the internal desire to be the **super black professor**. That image typically includes some combination of the following incredibly high expectations.

1. Super teacher: one who performs transformative and inspired teaching every day in the classroom, grades extensive writing assignments within forty-eight hours, and answers e-mails instantaneously.
2. Super colleague: one who is central to the functioning of the department, provides immediate and insightful reviews of colleagues' work, attends all functions, and whose labor nobody can live without.
3. Super researcher: one who changes disciplinary paradigms and shatters disciplinary boundaries with brilliant and prolific research.
4. Super role model: one whom all students of color can look up to, be mentored by, and rely on as a champion of their causes.
5. Super institutional change agent: one who serves on every search committee, diversity committee, and committee needing "diverse perspectives," and who works to change decades-long structural problems within their institution single-handedly.
6. Super community activist: one who attends community meetings, is actively working for justice outside the university, and whose research directly impacts social problems.

The first three expectations can occur among all perfectionist tenure-track faculty, but the last three tend to be specific to underrepresented groups. Although internal and external activism may be important to individual majority faculty, they can be both externally created and internally imposed expectations for black faculty. To be honest, we do not know any super black professors (people who do all of these things simultaneously). Not even Barack Obama fits all of these criteria at one time. So we want to suggest to any reader who feels that he or she must fit all these criteria: go ahead and consciously release yourself from the unrealistic expectation of being super black professor. Instead, try being gentle and realistic with yourself and acknowledge that it is impossible to do all of these things in your first year on the tenure track.

Strategy: rethink your career as a book with many chapters. Instead of imagining that you must do all of the things listed above at the same time, try visualizing your career as a book with many chapters. Hopefully, you will have a long career and, by picturing it over the long haul, you can better manage your expectations for the first six years because they are but one of the early chapters of that book. It is a chapter in which the main theme is likely to be academic writing and publication. But you can also imagine later chapters that have different and exciting themes. A future chapter could center on work to transform the climate of your institution. Another chapter could focus on becoming a master teacher. A later chapter could feature writing for a popular audience and becoming a public intellectual. And another chapter could focus on work in the community for social change. The order of the chapters of your book may be different, but the point is the same: you can achieve different things that are central to your professional life during different time periods. However, your ability to make those choices depends on the focus on writing and publication in your first chapter.

We love the above metaphor, with the idea of different chapters of your career having different central themes. But what we love most is how easy it is to say no to things that are not the focus of your work in the current chapter. Knowing that there will be a later chapter that focuses on teaching will allow you to accept the limited time you can spend on teaching while on the tenure track. The focus on popular writing in a future chapter will allow you to work guilt free on academic writing today. And believing that there will be later chapters that center on institutional and social change will allow you the freedom to say no to overwhelming commitments in the present.

Unclear goals. Ambivalence about or avoidance of writing can be grounded in larger unresolved life questions: Who am I? What is my purpose? And what am I doing with my life? We frequently work with black faculty who were guided onto the academic path because they were bright and engaged students or because they were enraged by social injustices and wanted to work for social change. Somehow, they never got the message that scholarship and activism are two different endeavors, and that the daily reality of life as a faculty member is dramatically different from the daily life of a community activist. They often manifest their ambivalence by avoiding writing and the production of research, which essentially sabotages their own possibilities for success. Whenever we meet faculty members who have been unproductive for several years, we ask them what they would do with their life if money were no object. We have heard answers to that question ranging from "AIDS activist" to "wedding planner." But rarely do we hear that they would read, write, and conduct research.

We bring up this particular psychological block because it is okay if you are in a tenure-track position and do not want to be an academic. It is okay if you are at a research-intensive university and have come to realize that you hate research. It is even okay if you are at a small liberal arts college and realize you despise teaching. It is okay precisely because you can make a change in the course of your career. But do so from a proactive stance as opposed to waiting until your own self-sabotage results in a denial of tenure so that you are pressured to find a new position or path in life.

Strategy: give yourself time to think about your purpose. If you are stuck and deeply resistant to writing and committing time to your research, it may be time for a little self-reflection. Try giving yourself permission to explore what is underlying your ambivalence, and the mental space to investigate the possibility that you may not be functioning because you do not really want to be an academic. If your passion lies in another area, then begin considering the full range of possibilities that exist for incorporating that dimension into your life. Is it possible to include your passion in your research agenda? Is it possible to engage in writing projects that do not fulfill your tenure requirements but feed your soul? Is it possible that you need to look for a job in another sector entirely? Do any of the three cases below sound similar to you?

Geoff was an assistant professor of marketing at a college of business in one of the top ten programs in the United States. His passion was the development of microbusiness in rural Nigeria. During the academic year, he conducted market research and wrote prolifically. During the summer, he and his three children traveled to Nigeria where he worked with several communities to connect villagers with lenders and assist in business development. Geoff also brought students with him to work with Nigerian community members (for which they received course credit). He became a symbol for his college's commitment to entrepreneurship and global connections. In this way, Geoff combined his passion, his research, and his teaching.

Unlike Geoff, Benita failed to publish anything in her first four years. She decided to spend a month keeping a journal that documented how she felt at various points in her workday. Benita realized quickly that she strongly disliked teaching, was uninterested in the specialized topic of her research, and was exhausted by her sixty-hour work weeks. Alternatively, she enjoyed the service work involved in planning lectures, conferences, and intellectual events; loved learning about different fields; and was gifted at grant writing. Because of an inheritance, she did not need the security of a tenured faculty position and decided she would be happier serving in an administrative capacity. When a job as director of an institute became available at another university in the area, Benita applied aggressively and got the job. She now works a clean forty hours a week doing what she loves, and enjoys her personal life the rest of the time.

When Julie was a graduate student at a large urban research-intensive university, she was lively and intellectually engaged. But three years into her first tenure-track job at a small college in a rural location, she was miserable, physically ill, and unproductive. After engaging in self-reflection, Julie realized that, although she had loved learning in graduate school, she did not enjoy teaching four courses a semester and was not interested in academic writing. What she missed most was working in the community, living in a diverse urban space, and feeling like her daily activities made a difference. At the end of her third year on the tenure track, Julie decided to take a job as director of a small nonprofit organization in the city where she had attended graduate school. After a year, her physical symptoms disappeared, and she wondered why she had remained in academe so long.

Prioritize, Prioritize, Prioritize!

In the five years that we have been working with black tenure-track faculty, we have found that developing healthy pathways to publication is one of the top challenges these faculty members face. We hear the same thing over and over again: faculty understand the importance of publishing their research to earning promotion and tenure; yet too few spend the necessary time on daily writing. They talk the talk, but don't walk the walk. Our hope is that this chapter has made the case that daily writing throughout your tenure-track years will help you to keep publication as your top priority, to feel less anxiety about your level of production, and to move projects forward and out the door. Creating accountability groups also contributes toward making this process less alienating and provides necessary social support and mentoring (we discuss these groups in Chapter 10). Each publication will provide you with an opportunity to share your work with others and contribute to the important debates and discourse in your field of specialization. In the next chapter, we will continue the theme of matching your priorities to time by discussing the art of efficient teaching and service.

Takeaway Tips

- Block out sixty minutes of time in your calendar each day for writing.
- Try using the Sunday meeting as a way to plan your week and prioritize your writing.
- Work toward identifying the technical errors and psychological blocks that are holding you back from explosive productivity.

Suggested Readings

Becker, Howard. (1998). *Tricks of the Trade: How to Think About Your Research While You're Doing It.* Chicago: University of Chicago Press.

Boice, Robert. (1989). "Procrastination, Busyness and Bingeing." *Behaviour Research and Therapy* 27: 605–611.

Boice, Robert. (1999). *Professors as Writers: A Self-Help Guide to Productive Writing.* New York: New Forums Press.

Gray, Tara. (2005). *Publish and Flourish: Become a Prolific Scholar.* Las Cruces: New Mexico State University Press.

Zerubavel, Eviatar. (1999). *The Clockwork Muse: A Practical Guide to Writing Theses, Dissertations, and Books.* Cambridge, MA: Harvard University Press.

7 | The Art of Efficient Teaching and Service

TEACHING is one of the greatest stressors facing new faculty members. It can cause anxiety for a variety of reasons, including the fact that it is the one place where new faculty members are "on-stage," being directly observed and evaluated by students and peers. Teaching also demands a great deal of time, especially during the early years. And because few graduate programs provide rigorous college-level teacher training and supervision for graduate students, too often learning how to teach collides with the multiple demands of the first few years on the tenure track. Consequently, it is of little surprise that the greatest stress factor reported by new faculty is that they spend the majority of their time on **teaching**, followed closely by **service**, and have little left for **research** and **writing**. This stress is compounded by the reality that, at most institutions, great teaching goes unrewarded, good teaching is sufficient, and even extraordinary teaching will not overcome a lack of research productivity.

Deborah, an assistant professor of criminology at a small private liberal arts college in a large Southern city, learned this reality the hard way. Because she had served only as a grader and teaching assistant in graduate school, Deborah's heavy teaching load was literally on-the-job training in teaching. Her college had recently raised the bar on research standards without any accompanying decrease in teaching load in order to improve their institutional ranking. To win tenure, Deborah was expected to publish a book and several articles. Because she spent her first three years barely surviving the four-four load, she had little time or energy left for research and writing. Although she received a wholly supportive third year review, questions about her scholarly productivity surfaced in her fifth year. Her chair was insistent that Deborah would need to have her book in print to be promoted, which sent her into panic mode. She had no idea how she could complete the manuscript, find a publisher, and get the book published by the end of the year. As she looked back on her first three years, Deborah felt frustrated that she had spent too much time on teaching and neglected the one thing—her book—that her tenure decision was hanging on.

Sadly, Deborah's case is all too familiar and illustrative of several problems plaguing black faculty. In graduate school, Deborah had received poor mentoring and no training on how to teach. This left her having to figure things out from the start all on her own. As a new faculty member, Deborah had no mentor in her department and the research expectations for tenure, which gradually increased over her probationary period, had been poorly communicated to her. The lack of support that Deborah received was not attributable to hostility from her colleagues, but rather to benign neglect. Nobody had lunch with her or pulled her aside to talk about priorities and time management. No one offered to watch her teach "off the record" as a way of giving constructive feedback, and no one provided kindly tips about how to manage student demands of varying types. Because Deborah was virtually on her own from the moment that her tenure clock starting ticking, there was too much to do and not enough time to do it by the time her tenure review was around the corner.

Kerry Ann can sympathize with Deborah because she began her career as an academic in similar ways. Kerry Ann accepted her first job at Henry Ford Community College (HFCC) shortly after defending her dissertation. This was a huge mistake that not a single person at her graduate institution advised her against. At HFCC, Kerry Ann taught five courses per semester, served on seven active committees, and held ten office hours per week as required by her union contract. Although the college did not expect her to produce any research in order to earn tenure, she had to collect survey and interview data, analyze it, and write her dissertation in order to complete her degree.

During her first year at HFCC, Kerry Ann collected no data and wrote nothing because she was learning how to teach in addition to serving on the seven committees and holding office hours. Her life revolved around committee meetings and her desperate attempt to manage five courses. When classes ended after her first year, Kerry Ann took a long hard look at herself and found she was a wreck! She was constantly running around like a chicken with its head cut off, literally sprinting from one commitment to another. She stayed up late at night writing lectures and grading even though she had to be up early to teach her 8:00 A.M. classes. The lack of sleep took a toll on her body, and she felt exhausted and demoralized most of the time. Kerry Ann had potential to be a great teacher, but she was trying to do too much in light of the number of classes she was teaching.

In addition to feeling as if her life was falling apart, Kerry Ann looked like a disaster to her colleagues. Every time they saw her, she was disheveled and running to her next fiasco. Papers were perpetually falling out of her bag, her hair was a tangled mess, and her clothes were wrinkled. Some of her students even felt the need to help their poor unkempt professor—one gave her a comb and some conditioner in a brown paper bag after class. If anyone asked Kerry Ann how she was doing, she spewed out all of her problems and occasionally cried. Though the rumpled, absent-minded professor image works for middle-aged white men, it gets read as "incompetent," "struggling," or "train wreck" for black faculty. One day during finals week of her first year, Kerry Ann came to work in the same clothing she had worn on the previous day, because she had overslept and grabbed the first thing on the floor. That morning, after a long glare up and down, one of her colleagues asked her, "Oh, dear, did you sleep in your office?" At that moment, Kerry Ann had to ask herself: how will I ever manage to complete my dissertation if I cannot even engage in proper grooming?

Kerry Ann's story is common and illustrates the ways that teaching-related stress manifests in the lives of new faculty who were never taught how to teach efficiently. Like many new professors, neither of us was properly mentored or supported in our first jobs and, as a result, we stumbled. It is important for you to know this because we are not writing from the position of having never made errors. Instead, it is quite the opposite. We both made many mistakes, and were embedded in situations that were not set up for us to succeed. Yet we were able to recover from those missteps and move on to successful management of our teaching and service. If we were able to move from unsuccessful first years into thriving careers, so can everyone who reads this book.

"Typical New Faculty Members"

Deborah and Kerry Ann are two examples of the "typical new faculty member" as described by Robert Boice (1992). In his research on faculty development and productivity, Boice found that the vast majority of new faculty exhibit the following characteristics:

- Go to class overprepared.
- Spend far less time on scholarly writing than what is necessary to meet promotion and tenure criteria.

- Teach defensively.
- Receive student evaluations that fall well below their expectations.
- Feel a sense of loneliness and a lack of collegial acceptance.

We will speak about each of these briefly because, even though they certainly hold true for the typical faculty member, they often are magnified for black faculty because of the ways that race and racism shape classroom dynamics.

Overpreparing for Class

Boice (1992) found that typical new faculty members come to class with far more material than they can realistically cover in a given class period. As a result, they rush to complete everything at the expense of active student participation. They get so caught up in trying to cram all of the material (which they stayed up all night to prepare) into one class period that they become oblivious to the students in their midst. In fact, among the new faculty that Boice studied, they averaged thirty hours per week on class preparation.

Even if teaching is your sole responsibility, thirty hours of course preparation + actual teaching time + office hours = more than a full-time job. It is no wonder that many faculty members in their first few years work sixty- to eighty-hour weeks. They put in a full forty-hour week on teaching, complete a myriad of service, and then try to squeeze in their research on top of all that. Why does this happen? Why do we spend so much time on teaching when, for most faculty, it has been made explicitly clear that teaching is not the most critical factor in promotion and tenure? Deborah and Kerry Ann experienced the same trap: the structure of classroom teaching created a built-in accountability mechanism. Few of us are willing to stand in front of a class unprepared day after day. Facing a class of undergraduates (and, even more so, graduate students) can be an anxiety-provoking experience that leads most junior faculty to overprepare as a way of avoiding the humiliation of blank stares, bored faces, or confused expressions.

Although overpreparation for classes affects most new faculty, it looks and feels different for black faculty. Why? Because, when students enter a classroom, they do not expect to see a black person as their professor and, therefore, black faculty simply do not get the benefit of the doubt from students. They have to prove their competence, as opposed to majority faculty who receive the benefit of the doubt until their behavior creates questions about competence. Most faculty experience anxiety walking into the classroom, but the experience is qualitatively different when you know up front that students do not necessarily assume you are competent, credentialed, or intellectually worthy of being in front of the classroom. The apprehension increases with the awareness that every mistake may be magnified, counted against you, and generalized to all black faculty. In short, many black faculty operate on the assumption that they will have to be twice as good in order to be evaluated as equal. This extra, invisible burden creates increased expectations to perform flawlessly in the classroom, leading to time-consuming overpreparation.

Talking the Talk, but Not Walking the Walk

In addition to overpreparation for class, typical new faculty members spend less time on scholarly writing than necessary to meet promotion and tenure criteria. This is fascinating because, on one hand, most faculty clearly articulate the importance of research in their promotion and tenure decision, completely understand that research and publication are a cumulative and slow process, and fully comprehend the quantity and quality of published work that is expected of them. But on the other hand, they spend little time each week on writing and research. The problem is the chasm between new faculty members' stated priorities and how they actually spend their time.

The disconnection between what individual faculty members believe is important to win tenure and how they spend their time is, once again, greater for black faculty than it is for white faculty. This is because the situation of being "the only" or "one of several" black faculty in a department, college, or university means that greater demands are placed on your time. Time pressures are created for black faculty that are simply not present for their majority colleagues because you may be asked to serve on a committee for every graduate student whose research is related to race, to serve on multiple institutional committees that require diverse representation, and to respond to ongoing requests from students of color who seek out the few black faculty as role models. Although we coach people to say no frequently, gracefully, and without guilt, the sheer regularity of having to figure out how to say no takes disproportionate time and energy. Whenever black faculty do not consciously attend to how they spend their time, they will find that there is less and less of it to spend on the items that are important to their promotion and tenure decisions.

Teaching Defensively

Boice (1992) found that typical new faculty go to great lengths to try to avoid student complaints. In doing so, they engage in what he refers to as "defensive teaching," which occurs when junior faculty are afraid of doing anything that might undermine their credibility. And in the case of black faculty, this might support preexisting student stereotypes that they are nothing more than "unqualified affirmative action hire." The result can be extraordinary measures to overcompensate both by over-preparing for class and by teaching in ways that tend to block students from having a chance to ask questions or participate in meaningful ways.

In the discussion above, Deborah spent hours preparing each lecture for a course and, by the time she actually got to class, she had prepared roughly two and a half hours of material for an eighty-minute class period. The same pattern unfolded for each class period. Deborah expected to wow her students with content, but instead discovered halfway through class that she had prepared too much material and had to race at a sprinter's pace to get through the remaining lecture. Students were unable to take notes at the fast pace, became exhausted from watching Deborah speed through the content, and eventually felt their eyes glaze over by the end of class. Everyone ended up unsatisfied. Deborah felt continually frustrated by the lack of class time and engagement of her students. Her students felt frustrated by Deborah's inability to plan and pace in a way that allowed their engagement.

New faculty often falsely believe that, if they cram a class period with content, students cannot ask questions or contradict, challenge, or expose any content errors. It is a fallacy to operate on the assumption that lots of material makes a great class and allows a professor to leave class feeling successful after simultaneously delivering that content while minimizing students' public complaints or questions. This is what Boice (1992) means by "defensive teaching," and it is problematic both because it is unenjoyable and because students do not evaluate great teaching in terms of the volume of content. Even more importantly, students must engage the material in order for learning to occur.

Disappointing Evaluations

That brings us to the inevitable disappointment that typical new faculty members experience when they receive their student evaluations. Boice (1992) found that most new faculty are deeply frustrated and confused by their student evaluations. In the face of disappointing evaluations, they tend to blame the results on everything but their teaching. They rationalize that the low numbers must be due to invalid rating systems, poor-quality students, unfavorable class times, or class sizes.

As with most evaluative factors, teaching evaluations are tricky for black faculty because of the way that race operates in the classroom. It is well documented that students' ratings of black faculty are lower, and that the factors they are evaluated on differ from those of white faculty. Most new faculty members are oriented to look externally for explanations of disappointing evaluations but, for black faculty, there indeed are external factors that matter and are out of their control.

Feelings of Loneliness and a Lack of Collegial Acceptance

It should come as no surprise that the frustrating cycle described above can leave a typical faculty member feeling lonely, unsupported, and disconnected from colleagues. Spending thirty hours a week preparing for courses leaves you alone most of the time. If you teach defensively and out of a place of fear, you are closed off to the possibilities of peer observation, student input, and other forms of constructive criticism. When you do not receive the evaluations you expect, feelings of defeat can make you unlikely to share them with colleagues. In the first years on the tenure track, any perception of failure can make it even more difficult to connect with colleagues who could provide you with the very guidance and support that you need.

The main point of Boice's (1992) research on typical new faculty members is that the common characteristics described above are widespread. Faculty development experts like Joann Moody would agree, and add to the discussion that there are additional extenuating characteristics associated with being a "solo" faculty member (the only woman, the only black person, etc.) and that the very circumstance of being "the only" creates unique obstacles. She argues that there are special stresses and extra taxes associated with solo status and that they are likely only to increase the already extant problem of loneliness and lack of acceptance felt by all new faculty.

Typical Faculty Versus Quick Starters

While Boice (1992) found that "typical" new faculty members experience an array of problems, not all new faculty have a difficult transition from graduate student to professor. Somewhere between 5 percent and 9 percent of new faculty emerge as "quick starters." In our experience, individual faculty who fit this description are referred to as "stars" or "the golden boy or golden girl." Quick starters hit the ground running in their new positions, where they turn out enough proposals and papers in their first two to three years to put them in fine shape for promotion and tenure. They score in the top quartile of peer and student ratings of teaching. And most importantly, they score in the top quartile of self-rated enjoyment and comfort levels as teachers.

Too often, the productivity of these individuals is attributed to their possession of superior natural abilities. They are described as "driven," "brilliant," or "a genius." But we would argue that these individuals are no more intelligent, motivated, or gifted than any other faculty member. They just spend their time in dramatically different ways. As Boice (1992) documents, quick starters differ from typical faculty in the following ways:

- Spend three hours or more per week on scholarly writing.
- Integrate their research into their undergraduate classes.
- Do not spend major amounts of time on course preparation (after their first semester, they averaged one to one and a half hours of preparation per lecture hour).
- Lecture at a pace that allows for active student participation.
- Regularly seek advice from colleagues, averaging four hours a week on discussions of research and teaching.

Given that each of these differences are behavioral (not genetic), it means that, with some basic behavior modification, any typical faculty member can become a quick starter. The key to this transition is **balance**.

A Balance Program for Black Faculty

Boice's (1992) research yielded an approach to help new faculty avoid common pitfalls and become quick starters. His balance program consists of a few simple steps that can assist faculty as they transition from graduate student to professor. We have taken this basic structure and modified it for black academics in order to transform new faculty of color from typical faculty members to quick starters with only a small number of changed behaviors.

Step 1: Limit Classroom Preparation to a Maximum of Two Hours per Hour of Lecture

Although this is inconceivable for most faculty at first, Boice (1992) reports success for those who are willing to try it. New faculty are surprised to find that they can still cover the material that they want while appearing more relaxed in front of their students and teaching at a pace that encourages active student involvement. Below are some concrete ways that faculty have used to successfully limit their class preparation time.

Align your personal standards with your department's standards. Having too high expectations for your class can result in spending too much time preparing. New faculty sometimes arrive with far higher standards for content and rigor than are normative in their department. Examine your colleagues' syllabi, talk to them about what it means to teach a 100-level course at your particular institution, and ask your peers if you can visit their classrooms. Then bring your teaching standards and practices into alignment with the departmental norms.

Use standardized assessments. Find out what types of evaluation mechanisms are common and acceptable in your department. If the norm is to give multiple-choice exams, then relieve yourself of any guilt about giving multiple-choice exams. If the norm is to give writing assignments, talk to your colleagues about how intensively they grade them (and ask for examples). If you teach writing-intensive courses, consider having students work on a single piece that they revise regularly over the semester, as opposed to producing multiple different papers. Figure out how you can devise rubrics for grading that will allow other people to grade assignments.

Hire a grader, graduate assistant, or undergraduate teaching assistant. Whenever possible, get assistance with your teaching. Graduate assistants and teaching assistants can save you a great deal of time as long as you are clear about your tasks and are willing to delegate. If you do not have the luxury of having a teaching assistant assigned to your class, you need to get creative. For example, we regularly ask the top students in our undergraduate courses to be "undergraduate teaching assistants" in the same course in the following semester. Offer the students independent study credit for their efforts. Require them to meet with you each week, complete reading about college teaching, and assist with the nonessential tasks in the class. This works well because it costs you nothing, the undergraduate is typically honored and delighted by the invitation, and it provides a better overall class experience for your students.

Delegate, delegate, and delegate some more. There are some tasks associated with teaching that only you can do, and there are many more tasks that can be done by anyone. The trick is to know the difference. For example, making copies, grading multiple-choice exams, and updating a grade spreadsheet or gradebook are not things that require your individual attention. Preparing a lecture, giving a lecture, and facilitating discussion are things that only you can do. Separating out the two allows you to delegate the nonessential tasks to a teaching assistant and decrease your preparation time.

Get organized. Disorganization translates into time wasted searching for information, papers, and the other things you need to do your job. If you make an effort on the front end to develop a functional organizing system, your physical space will be maximized for efficiency and you will save an enormous amount of time because your files will allow you to retrieve what you need when you need it.

Use lesson plans. We encourage faculty to develop lesson plans for their courses for three simple reasons. First, a lesson plan forces you to clarify a learning objective for a specific class period (what students should be able to do by the end of your one-hour meeting). Second, a lesson plan is an organizational tool. You need to write a plan only one time. After that, you can go back to find that everything is right there for you to review quickly before teaching the same class the following year. Finally, a lesson plan is a tool to assist in delegation. Ask your teaching assistant to pull the files for the next two weeks of class, examine the lesson plans, and make any necessary arrangements for additional materials (outside media, handouts, slides, etc.). Next, request that the teaching assistant place the file that you will need for each class day in your in-box, along with the materials. You can then come to your office shortly before class, review what is necessary, and go off to class with minimal time spent.

Avoid teaching when possible. The most efficient way to reduce your teaching time is to find creative ways not to teach. We both love teaching, but we still seek out ways to be released from teaching at times. We strongly encourage tenure-track faculty to ask for a teaching load reduction during their first year (as part of their initial negotiations), apply for internal and external fellowships in their first three years on the tenure track, write course releases into grant proposals, and explore resourceful ways to reduce their teaching load (that are in line with their institutional culture), such as (1) requesting a teaching release in exchange for large and extraordinary service requests, (2) team teaching, and (3) asking for one large course to count as two smaller ones.

Step 2: Write Daily

We have already said several times in this book that the people who are productive in their writing are those who write daily. But it bears repeating because there is a pervasive myth among new faculty that they must find long unbroken stretches of time to write. Let's get real. This is a myth precisely because nobody who is spending thirty hours a week preparing for class + teaching + committee work + life is going to have the luxury of large blocks of time to write. Daily writing leads to slow, but steady, productivity. More importantly, it leads to reduced feelings of anxiety over failure to meet scholarly productivity expectations. In other words, if you write daily, you will never again end a semester empty-handed.

Boice (1992) found that the quick starters all wrote for small periods of time on a regular basis. We have made numerous suggestions in Chapter 10, "Building a Supportive Network," about how you can develop systems of support and accountability for your writing that are similar to those that are automatically built into teaching and service. But if you are one of those faculty who believe it is not possible to set aside an hour at the beginning of each day to write, ask yourself: why not? Then, figure out what you are afraid might happen if you do make these changes and what will happen if you do not put your highest priority first, engage in daily writing, and reduce time spent on your teaching or service.

Step 3: Integrate Research Interests into Teaching

One of the most effective strategies to reduce preparation time and integrate the various components of your position into a whole is to infuse the courses that you teach with your research interests. This will work because you know your research area better than anything else and, if you love what you do, it will be conveyed to your students through greater enthusiasm and energy. This has the extra positive impact of making it possible for you to recruit research assistants in the future if students find your work as interesting as you do.

We recognize that combining research and teaching is easier in some disciplines than others, but we especially encourage those who think this is impossible to seek out colleagues who do so effectively and figure out how they do it. Nearly every department has a faculty member who is widely known as a superstar in the classroom. Figure out who that is in your department, invite him or her to coffee, and ask for specifics about how to engage students and bring your research into the classroom. We often give this as homework to the faculty whom we coach (especially when they swear that it is impossible to bring the complex research of their field into the undergraduate classroom). Inevitably, they return to their next session with inspiration from colleagues' success in this area and the realization that they need to learn how to ask for help.

Step 4: Devote Four Hours Weekly to Discuss Teaching and Research with Colleagues

In a perfect world, new faculty would be warmly welcomed into their departments and senior faculty would extend themselves to develop supportive and nurturing relationships. Unfortunately, we do not live in a perfect world, so you cannot sit back waiting for people to come to you and being resentful when that does not happen. Instead, be proactive and invite people to casual, but substantive, discussions with you about teaching and research. One way to do this is by asking people to lunch. It does not matter whether lunch means bringing brown bags to the conference room or sharing a meal at a faculty dining room or restaurant; just go with the norms of your institution. If lunch seems like too much, try a coffee or tea break. If you are a shy person, this will be difficult at first, but the long-term payoff is well worth it.

In initiating these conversations, you cannot expect any one person to emerge as your guru mentor. Instead, take a step back to look at the senior faculty in your department and think seriously about what you can learn from each one of them. If they are great teachers, then consider them to be "teaching mentors." If they have an extraordinarily successful research program, consider them a "research mentor." If they are an opinion leader within the institution or the professional organizations in your discipline, then consider them a "professional development mentor." Remember that (1) you most likely will have to take the first step, (2) you can learn something from everyone in your department, and (3) you will gain a lot by proactively structuring these conversations on a regular basis.

Step 5: Keep Daily Records of Work Time Expenditure

Recording the amount of time that you spend on various activities is about as enjoyable as sitting in the dentist's chair. However, it will help you accomplish two important skills. The first is that you will begin to learn how long various tasks actually take. How long does it take to grade twenty-five essay exams? How long does it take to prepare a lecture from scratch? How long does it take to organize your paperwork weekly? How long does it take to meet with a teaching assistant to delegate tasks? Understanding how much time is taken by various tasks can help you to plan better in the future. More importantly, tracking your time allows you to determine on a weekly basis how well you are meeting your commitments. If you keep track of how your time is spent, you can honestly answer the big questions about how much time you have spent on teaching, service, research, and relationship building in any given week and over the period of a semester.

To be clear, this is the least exciting part of Boice's (1992) balance program and the one that most faculty deem right off the top as unnecessary and unpleasant. To us, it is similar to the general reluctance to track how we spend our money. This resistance often emerges from an unwillingness to reconcile the truth of our behavior with an imagined sense of where our money goes. Facing the reality of our monetary spending is frequently full of surprises—we cannot believe how much money was spent in areas where we thought we were frugal. The same principle of surprise holds for time expenditures. Rarely do we coach faculty who hold an accurate assessment of how they spend their time, how long specific tasks take, or how much their priorities and actual behavior disagree. Although painful, reconciling these differences will allow you to live in a professional state of honesty and pinpoint the areas in which you can improve.

Following the balance program is not a quick and easy fix. In fact, it is incredibly difficult for most faculty. Boice's group resisted the changes, defended their routine ways of working despite their unhappiness, and required regular meetings with a mentor to help them stay with the program. Faculty members especially resisted limiting lecture preparation time. But Boice followed faculty over time who agreed (however reluctantly) to try his program. After only five weeks of limiting preparation time, daily writing, integrating their research into teaching, proactively discussing research and teaching with colleagues, and tracking time, they began to both look and feel more like quick starters. After a while, they attained the standards set out in the plan, reported greater efficiency in their teaching, and reported higher levels of comfort in their teaching.

For junior faculty with no support, changing behavior takes considerable effort. However, by applying practical constraints on teaching and service, it is possible to balance them with research. This alignment of priorities and time in each of these areas lowers stress and increases job satisfaction. Also, the release of anxiety that many junior faculty experience simply by writing every day is transformative, and the substantive conversations with your colleagues can lead to enhanced relationships that will make the initial discomfort and struggle of reaching out well worth it.

The N-Word

While Boice's (1992) research is mainly concerned with helping new faculty teach efficiently and increase the time available for research, black faculty often face tremendous time demands from service requirements. With the best of intentions, white faculty often advise faculty of color to just say no. At the surface level, this is exactly what you must do. But at a deeper level, this seemingly simple advice too often fails to acknowledge the sheer volume of requests that the average black faculty member receives over and above majority faculty. It neglects the complex equation of work you may feel obligated to do on top of research and teaching, and the differential costs associated with saying no to various administrators' requests for participation in a never-ending stream of diversity work. Because we acknowledge that just saying no is more complicated for black faculty than it appears, we want to extend the discussion of Boice's balance program by providing some guidelines for evaluating service requirements and requests.

First and foremost, we encourage all black faculty to take the time to understand why you say yes to service requests. Is it simply a knee-jerk response? Do you want to please the person asking you? Are you feeling guilty about some other aspect of your work that you want to make up for? Are you trying to right the long-standing historical and structural inequalities of your institution? Are you trying to single-handedly make up for all the systemic failures that your students have experienced in their academic careers? Do you feel like you must say yes or you will be punished for saying no? Is that fear self-created or is it real? We advise faculty never to say yes to any service request on the spot. If someone asks you for your time, create some time for yourself to think about it by saying, "I need to consult my calendar and workload before I can say yes or no. I'll get back to you tomorrow." Then, consult your strategic plan, calendar, and weekly workload and ask yourself why you might say yes, but also give yourself permission to say no.

Too often, black faculty feel that they must be all things to all people right out of the gate. We must be the role model and super teacher for students of color, the super adviser and research mentor for our graduate students, the super departmental citizen to our colleagues to prove they made the right choice in hiring us, and we also must work toward changing the institution we are embedded in. These intentions are admirable and, at the height of your career, you may look back to see that you have accomplished every one of them. However, it is impossible to do all of these things in your first, second, or third year on the tenure track. And if any of these expectations are precluding you from research, writing, and publication, you will not be at your institution long enough for your efforts to matter. Take a look at your career from a long-term perspective or, as previously suggested, as a book with many chapters. Some chapters will be focused on research, some will emphasize teaching, and others will focus on institutional change. If you give yourself permission to focus in your tenure-track years on what is going to win you tenure and promotion, be assured that you are not eliminating other goals but instead are spreading them out over your career.

Ten Ways to Say No

Saying no effectively means being clear and assertive. There are multiple ways to say no, and you can choose how you want to do so in any context and interpersonal relationship. By way of example, we offer the following ten ways to say no that range in sentiment and forcefulness:

1. That sounds like a really great opportunity, but I just cannot take on any additional commitments at this time.
2. I am not comfortable with that _____ (situation, task, group of people involved).
3. I feel overwhelmed by service right now, so I am going to have to decline your generous invitation.
4. I am in the middle of _____, _____, and _____ and, if I hope to get tenure, I am unable to take on any additional service.
5. I am not the best person for this. Why don't you ask _____?
6. If you can find a way to eliminate one of my existing service obligations, I will consider your request.
7. I would rather say no to your request than do a halfhearted job on the committee.
8. Right now, I need to focus on my research agenda and publication. When I have tenure, I hope to be able to say yes to requests like this one.
9. I cannot serve on your committee right now. But why don't you ask me again next year?
10. No. (Look the asker in the eye and sit in silence.)

We titled this chapter "The Art of Efficient Teaching and Service" because aligning your priorities and time, teaching efficiently, and learning to say no effectively are an art form. Yet they can be easily mastered and executed as long as you remain conscious of your behavior, question the underlying reasons that you do the things you do, and are patient with yourself as you grow into your new role as a professor.

Takeaway Tips

- The difference between typical new faculty and quick starters is how they spend their time.
- To become a quick starter, limit class preparation to two hours per hour of lecture, write daily, integrate research interests into your teaching, spend four hours per week talking about research and teaching with your colleagues, and keep track of how you spend your time.
- Say no often and without guilt, knowing that you are receiving more requests because of your status as a black faculty member.
- Never agree to a service request on the spot—buy yourself time by saying you will consult your calendar.
- Develop a list of creative ways to say no.

Suggested Readings

Bain, Ken. (2004). *What the Best College Teachers Do*. Cambridge, MA: Harvard University Press.

Boice, Robert. (1992). *The New Faculty Member: Supporting and Fostering Professional Development*. San Francisco: Jossey-Bass.

Lang, James. (2005). *Life on the Tenure Track: Lessons from the First Year*. Baltimore: Johns Hopkins University Press.

McKeachie, Wilbert J. (1999). *Teaching Tips: Strategies, Research, and Theory for College and University Teachers* (10th ed.). New York: Houghton Mifflin.

Moody, JoAnn. (2004). *Faculty Diversity: Problems and Solutions*. New York: Routledge.

PART 3

Playing to Win

8 | Shifting from Habits of Survival to Strategies for Success

FOR black faculty on the road to tenure, the challenge of winning tenure without losing your soul is situated against the backdrop of racial oppression. All junior faculty members occupy a one-down status within the institutional hierarchy as tenure-track professors. For black faculty, the role-specific one-down status of being "junior" is compounded by racism. Because you do not fit the traditional professorial mold, you do not receive the benefit of the doubt, and must do twice as much to be considered equal. As a black academic, you are especially vulnerable to internalizing your department's values as your own, evaluating your self-worth according to those values, and losing your integrity in the desperate attempt to prove you are good enough and deserve to receive permanent membership in the club.

The risk of losing your soul is tied to a double bind that is inherent in the anatomy of oppression. This **double bind** refers to the dilemma of being doomed no matter what you do. For black academics, the double bind creates a situation whereby you can "choose" to push back and resist injustice in your institutional context, but this can lead to professional destruction (denial of tenure). Alternatively, you can "choose" to submit to injustice to avoid retaliation and punishment, but doing so comes at the cost of spiritual destruction (losing your soul). We put the word "choose" in quotations because we consider these to be problematic choices or false choices in the sense that both options render a similar fate, namely, some form of destruction. Of course, the term *destruction* sounds dramatic and we realize that not all situations involve such extreme consequences. Nevertheless, whatever the matter of degree may be, the reality is that many black academics find themselves trapped in a double bind whereby whatever they do, they are faced with some form of loss. It can be the loss of professional opportunities, rewards, and advancement (with the ultimate consequence being the loss of tenure) or the loss of your voice and the space to directly assert your truths (in other words, the loss of personal integrity and your soul). Consequently, when all possible choices render some form of loss, there really is no genuine choice to be made, only the choice of what type of loss you are willing to endure.

We begin this chapter by outlining the habits of survival.[1] These are ways that individual black faculty have learned to cope with oppression in various institutional contexts. You will most likely recognize yourself, and many of your colleagues, as we describe these mechanisms of survival. We describe them in detail so you can become conscious of the unconscious coping mechanisms that have helped you to survive throughout your academic career. To be clear, our ultimate goal is to move from only surviving on the tenure track to thriving as black academics. In order to do so, you not only need to understand how you have survived in the past, but also learn the strategies necessary to succeed within institutions that were not designed for your success.

Habits of Survival

To manage the stress that comes from living within an oppressive and adverse environment, many minorities develop **habits of survival**. These are rigidified and automatic ways of being that develop in response to oppression and pervade every aspect of your lived experience. The nature of a habit is that it is neither conscious nor chosen. It is a way of being that a person assumes automatically, and its purpose is to help that individual negotiate and endure in the face of oppressive conditions. Habits of survival are a dominant stance (or a way of being) that is defined by an organizing mental framework. They include specific mechanisms for channeling the rage and frustration that inevitably arise in response to oppression and a set of core behavioral tendencies.

Habits of survival have both functional and dysfunctional dimensions. The functional dimensions of habits of survival are that they are adaptive responses to oppression. They arise as a way of helping those who are oppressed to negotiate life within an adverse environment so they can endure in spite of the forces pressing down on them. Habits, by definition, are automatic and rigidified so they help oppressed people to conserve energy. Given the extraordinary stressors and strains imposed by the forces of oppression, learning to conserve energy is critical.

While habits of survival have functional elements, they also have dysfunctional aspects. Because they are automatic and rigidified, they are invoked repetitively, under all circumstances, irrespective of whether or not they are best suited to the situation at hand. Inevitably, there are some circumstances that call for ways of being, thinking, and behaving that are outside the parameters of a given habit of survival. Yet the automatic nature of habits of survival prevents individuals from reflexively evaluating how to respond in a particular situation. This limits adaptation and growth and undermines conscious choice and decisionmaking.

Choice is critical to freedom and liberation. To be free is to be able to choose how you will live your life. The nature of oppression is that it deprives people of the freedom to exercise choices. Oppression imposes a double bind such that you are doomed to destruction no matter what choices you make. If you submit to the forces that are trying to hold you down, you become a participant in your psychological and spiritual erasure and demise. On the other hand, if you resist and fight back, you are likely to encounter a more direct and literal form of destruction (e.g., economic, professional, physical). In either case, the outcome is destruction, which means there really is no choice, only a false choice.

In response to this false choice, many develop habits of survival that are grounded in avoiding the form of destruction that they perceive to be the most threatening. For some, psychological or spiritual destruction is more terrifying than physical destruction; for others, the reverse is true. Whichever form of destruction is more frightening determines the habit of survival an individual develops. Even the particular habit of survival we adopt is not a matter of a conscious choice, but driven by our fears and insecurities. These compel us to assume a habit of survival without actually making a conscious decision about it. There are five prototypical habits of survival. Others may in fact exist, but based on our research with oppressed populations, we regard these five as core habits of survival: (1) subservience, (2) the warrior, (3) feigned subservience, (4) the oppressed oppressor, and (5) cultural splitting. We discuss each habit and encourage you to consider which one (if any) best describes your own response to oppression.

The Subservience Habit of Survival

Black faculty who adopt the **subservience habit of survival** take a one-down stance in response to oppression. Their organizing mental framework is that it is not safe to resist or challenge authority or injustice.

Their position toward racism and inequalities at their college or university can be summed up as follows: "I just have to accept that this is the way things are." As a result, the rage and frustration that are associated with oppression are directed inwardly toward the self. The behavioral tendencies associated with the subservience habit include:

- Suppressing or denying your needs or not even knowing what your needs are.
- Rationalizing unpleasant realities.
- Engaging in self-destructive, self-deprecating, or self-sacrificing behaviors (e.g., addictions, eating disorders, staying in abusive relationships).

Because faculty who assume the subservience habit acquiesce to domination, often they are able to minimize the direct wrath of the oppressor. Their orientation toward compliance and placation makes them behave in ways that are pleasing to those with power. As a result, faculty members with the subservience habit frequently receive institutional benefits as a result of their compliance. They are seen as highly collegial and they "get along with others." At the same time, there are dysfunctional dimensions of the subservience habit. First, because they have difficulty recognizing who the oppressor is, they are highly susceptible to acting aggressively against themselves. For example, self-destructive patterns of behavior like substance abuse or eating disorders are common. Second, because they find it almost impossible to resist the forces of oppression that press down on them, they become complicit in their own subjugation, which inflicts a blow to their psyche. Finally, by assuming a consistently deferential stance, those with this habit are sometimes made more vulnerable to abuse from oppressors because their passivity arouses (rather than pacifies) the aggression of those who hold more power.

Although the behaviors that are characteristic of this habit are heavily oriented around deference toward others and denial of one's needs, in reality no one is purely deferential and self-denying. To some degree, each of us has a place of resistance within us. In the case of those who assume the subservience habit, embedded within their self-destructive behaviors are private acts of rebellion. In a perverse way, the very behaviors that represent denial of the self are also acts of empowerment. For example, drug addiction is often associated with the subservience habit.

Those who develop a dependency on drugs are engaging in self-destructive behaviors that involve turning their rage inward, suppressing their voice, and attempting to avoid unpleasant realities by retreating into a cloud of anesthesia. Yet at the same time, this behavior also can be understood as a private form of rebellion, a covert way of pushing back against pain and injustice. Addictions to alcohol or food, for example, involve denying rage and pain, yet also constitute a way of expressing rage and pain. There is no doubt that addictions to alcohol or food are destructive, but it is critical to recognize the seed of functionality within the soil of dysfunction. Although largely hurtful, some small sliver of this behavior reflects a piece of the self that has not given up entirely and is struggling against the odds to hang in and survive despite overwhelming pain, rage, and suffering.

Sandra was an assistant professor in the humanities who received her PhD from an Ivy League university in the late 1990s. Quiet and introverted, she was described as "brilliant" by those who took the time to read her work. Sandra started her position at a large state university when she was still "all but dissertation" and struggled to complete her dissertation, not finishing the degree until the end of her second year. Through the advocacy of her department chair, Sandra's tenure clock did not start until the beginning of her third year.

Sandra was extremely deferential with all of her colleagues, who were almost all middle-aged white men. Many of them treated her disrespectfully, frequently interrupting and correcting her. Unfortunately, their behavior was fueled by the fact that Sandra never challenged them. Even when they made thinly veiled sexist and racist comments in her presence, or to her directly, she remained meek and submissive. A few were supportive of her and tried to mentor her. In these relationships, she worked hard to be pleasing. For example, she set aside her own work to provide in-depth feedback on a paper for a senior colleague who was under pressure to meet a deadline.

Because Sandra found the interactions with most of her colleagues to be unpleasant, she tried to avoid them as much as possible. For example, she rarely made eye contact with her departmental colleagues in the elevator or when she passed them in the hallways. If someone spoke to her, she avoided their gaze and frequently looked down. She tried to avoid faculty meetings and, when she did attend, she arrived late and sat in silence in the outer ring of chairs that surrounded the main table. In fact, she went to campus only when she had to teach or attend a meeting.

One of Sandra's strengths was that she was extremely active in the area of service. She sat on numerous committees and mentored many students of color. Because she found it difficult to say no to anyone, and because she genuinely cared about students, she either advised or sat on the committee of almost every black graduate student in the department. Despite her high level of behind-the-scenes activity, Sandra's disinclination toward self-promotion left her colleagues largely unaware of her service load. Ironically, most senior faculty believed she was not "pulling her weight" and was unfairly relieved of service because she was the department's lone black professor. In terms of her scholarship, Sandra was completely paralyzed. Although she told her chair that she was working while she was home, in reality she was not. She was not writing and had no energy for her research or much of anything. During her third year review, Sandra had no publications, no book contract, and she had made no progress on moving her manuscript from dissertation to book. Sandra's reviewers made it clear to her that she needed to publish in order to get promoted and win tenure. Although Sandra knew they were correct, she insisted that her writing was a "slow process," that she was working hard and moving forward, and that she would complete her book soon. But the truth was that Sandra was immobilized and unsure how to move forward. Also, unbeknownst to most everyone, Sandra had become dependent on alcohol as a way of mediating her anxiety and stress.

The struggles Sandra faced were numerous. Because of her submissive demeanor and avoidance of direct conflict with others, she was rarely subject to punitive actions from those who had power over her. However, many of her colleagues took her demeanor as license to treat her disrespectfully, and even her supporters were prone to taking advantage of her eagerness to please. While those who had taken the time to become acquainted with Sandra generally liked her, most did not know her and misinterpreted her distance as aloofness. Anything but aloof, it was Sandra's sense of caring for students and her inability to say no that had led her to overextend her self on service-related commitments. Moreover, Sandra's anxiety and doubt about her competence and self-worth had paralyzed her research agenda and was severely undermining her scholarly productivity. In some ways, she had never expected to get that far, but the stakes had become higher than ever before. Unfortunately, she was stuck in a self-defeating cycle: the less research she performed, the more critical others were of her. With each criticism, Sandra became more convinced of her incompetence and that reinforced her lack of productivity. To make matters worse, her dependency on alcohol, which grew out of her deeply rooted fears and insecurities, had become a problem in its own right.

Inevitably, Sandra's submissiveness was a product of many factors, but the significance of race and gender cannot be minimized. Sandra grew up in a family where her parents did not assert themselves in the face of racial offenses. On more than one occasion, she had observed her parents being disrespected by white people whom they failed to confront. She particularly remembered an incident when she was seven years old and her mother's employer, a white woman, made a racially derogatory remark that Sandra's mother did not confront. Sandra remembered feeling angry with her mother because, in Sandra's mind, she concluded that her mother was to blame for what had happened. Sandra deduced that her mother remained silent because she somehow must have deserved it. That underlying assumption played a powerful role in shaping Sandra's feelings about herself as a black woman and how she fashioned her stance in the world. Watching her parents' deference in the face of racial offenses socialized Sandra to be similarly deferential. Moreover, her early experiences contributed to her willingness to overlook being disrespected by others and her tendency to blame herself rather than holding others accountable.

The Warrior Habit of Survival

Black faculty who assume the **warrior habit of survival** adopt an active, open resistance to oppression. They are clear about who the oppressor is and they are solidly committed to challenging that person or group, at any cost. Their organizing mental framework for viewing the world is refusing to humble themselves to any form of injustice and domination. This can be summed up in the following way: "I am not going to be beaten. I will fight until I overcome no matter what." Faculty members who develop the warrior habit direct the rage and frustration associated with oppression outward by resisting oppression at all times. The behavioral tendencies associated with the warrior habit are:

- Working tirelessly on behalf of "causes" or "missions."
- Occupying positions of leadership (usually within alternative and nonmainstream organizations).
- Having few, if any, truly intimate relationships or close connections.
- Constantly being in battle mode and therefore rarely taking time to stop and "smell the roses."

Both the functional and dysfunctional aspects of the warrior habit are related to the appropriate and intense direction of energy toward the source of oppression. Those who assume this habit tend to be excellent leaders because of their tenacious commitment to transforming unjust conditions. They are skilled at inspiring and calling others to action and at organizing collective energy aimed at challenging conditions of injustice and oppression. However, because most mainstream or traditional organizations and institutions (e.g., colleges and universities) manifest power through domination and are aligned with the status quo politics that reinforces the dynamics of oppression, those with the warrior habit are unlikely to advance to leadership positions within these systems. Instead, their leadership tends to be centered in community organizations outside of their home institution.

Those who adopt the warrior habit also tend to have difficulty being close with others. They fear being vulnerable because this has the potential to distract them from their cause. Intimacy places them at risk for being hurt or exploited by others, so they feel it is safer to keep their armor on at all times. As a result, those with the warrior habit tend to experience alienation and isolation from others, difficulty in sustaining intimate relationships, and accusations of being unable to "turn it off" when they are with friends and family.

Derrick was an assistant professor in a professional school at a large state university. He was passionate about his work, had high energy, and was clear about his radical politics. Derrick grew up in the large city where he currently worked. He was described by others as an organic, hip-hop, antiestablishment, revolutionary intellectual and community organizer who was more committed to the politics of the organizations he worked with than to the university agenda. Derrick had shoulder-length dreadlocks, and typically wore baggy pants and a T-shirt. He spent half of his twelve-hour workdays on campus and the other half in the offices and meetings of various community groups. Most of Derrick's colleagues found his profanity-laced Ebonics, his appearance, and his combative behavior reprehensible. Yet Derrick's publication record was impressive, and his frequent guest lectures at other institutions had helped to earn him a solid national reputation in his field. Importantly, Derrick had several high-status allies in his department: a cluster of senior white liberals who considered him to somehow represent black authenticity and a dean who was willing to defend him at any cost.

Derrick frequently ran into trouble at his institution because he let no subtle slight go unmentioned, no discussion go by without weighing in, and no informational e-mail go unchallenged. He fought every fight, created some fights that did not exist, and indiscriminately attacked his allies as often as his enemies. He was especially vigilant about racial issues and never hesitated to confront colleagues, students, and administrators for racial insensitivities and slights. For this reason in particular,

Derrick had more institutional enemies than allies, which he understood and accepted. Although he was solidly committed to his career success, he saw himself as fighting for a larger cause, and he was willing to endure whatever punishments might be inflicted on him for his unwavering commitment to racial justice.

The struggle Derrick faced was that he had virtually no life outside of his career and his work on behalf of social justice. He routinely worked twelve hours a day, seven days a week, and, as a result, he suffered from bouts of exhaustion. Although Derrick had an enormous network of acquaintances, he had few close relationships and found it difficult to sustain long-term relationships with girlfriends. Even though there were many who would have liked to be closer to him, Derrick managed to evade intimate contact with almost everyone. When challenged about his relational patterns, he claimed to want intimacy, but also declared that he did not have the time or energy for deep relationships. Truthfully, he feared that closeness with others would make him too vulnerable and even distracted from his professional and sociopolitical goals.

The Feigned Subservience Habit of Survival

Among black faculty, some adopt the **feigned subservience habit of survival**. In contrast to the subservience habit previously described, these faculty assume a fake one-down or deferential stance in response to oppression. Their organizing mental framework is summed up in the following way: "It is not safe to openly resist oppression, so I will pretend to accept things the way they are while covertly resisting at all times." This habit of survival represents an integration of the subservience and warrior habits. On the surface, these faculty appear similar to those adopting a subservience habit but, behind the scenes, they quietly but aggressively resist like their warrior colleagues. For black faculty who employ this habit, the rage and frustration associated with oppression are appropriately, although covertly, directed at the oppressor in the following ways:

- Having an outward appearance of deference. However, on closer examination, it is clear that these behaviors are shaded with nuances of mockery and exaggerated placating.
- Engaging in covert acts of resistance.
- Having a general mistrust of others that interferes with closeness and intimacy.
- Being skillful at negotiating systems and circumstances to sidestep direct pressures from those in power.

The functional aspects of the feigned subservience habit are that it enables faculty members to resist the conditions of oppression while sidestepping institutional retaliation from the powers that be. Black faculty who have developed the feigned subservience habit are skillful at working organizational systems to pursue their agendas. Because they do so in secrecy, they tend to succeed even when the odds are stacked against them. Therefore, they experience satisfaction in being able to successfully manipulate the system and realize the resultant direct, concrete rewards.

As with each habit of survival, there are both functional and dysfunctional aspects. Those adopting the feigned subservience habit tend to be highly mistrusting and suspicious of others, and thus have difficulty allowing others to get close to them. Their daily reliance on tactics of manipulation feeds mistrust and alienation in close relationships. Because so much of their existence is founded around secrecy and hidden agendas, they fear discovery and exposure, and assume others may be just as calculating and untrustworthy as they are.

Marissa was an assistant professor in the social sciences at the beginning of her fourth year at a large state university. As an ethnographer, Marissa had been trained to carefully observe her environment from the periphery to determine the cultural norms and values at work in an organization. In fact, Marissa had learned these skills long before she entered graduate school. As a black person raised in a predominantly white setting, she had survived by developing a feigned subservience habit of survival. This habit honed her ability to meticulously study her surroundings and develop strategies for appearing to comply with the expectations of a given context. When Marissa started on the tenure track at her university, she quickly applied these skills to her academic department. She realized early on that "getting along" was highly valued in her department because another junior colleague who had lodged justified complaints was quickly ostracized and labeled a "troublemaker." Moreover, as the only black person in her department, Marissa was further convinced that her survival depended on her ability to play along with her appointed role as a "congenial junior colleague." She did this by soliciting a lot of advice, never complaining, and making only supportive comments during faculty meetings. Marissa was perceived by her colleagues as a collegial junior faculty member, reliable departmental citizen, and productive scholar. Because Marissa's habit of survival was feigned subservience, her hidden truth was that she really did not want the advice she solicited and, although she never vocalized complaints, she harbored a multitude of them—many of which were about the racist behavior of her colleagues. She found a lot of her colleagues trifling, disagreed with many of the decisions her department made, and resented the numerous racial slights she had encountered during her four years. However, given the way that other junior faculty who complained had been punished and her racial isolation in the department, she elected to keep her genuine thoughts and feelings tucked away from public view.

Although Marissa had not publicly expressed her resistance, she found ways to push back subtly. For example, when Marissa was on a committee that made a decision she disagreed with, she offered to write the policy document that put the decision in writing. Marissa was highly organized and detail oriented in a department of disorganized and big-picture colleagues so the committee welcomed her offer. In writing the document, she retained the spirit of the decision, but removed several key aspects of it. Marissa knew that, by the time her colleagues read it again at a faculty meeting, they likely would have forgotten the details. She was correct. Marissa's version of the document was discussed at a faculty meeting four weeks after the committee made its initial decision and it was unanimously approved with little discussion. She had succeeded in removing most of the ugliness from the final product. Marissa was able to manage her professional relationships in a way that created a positive impression among her colleagues but secretly express her disagreements in ways that were invisible, yet effective.

The struggle Marissa faced, however, was that she did not trust any of her colleagues; therefore, she was not authentically engaged and felt disconnected at work. She hid this well, but she paid the price for this internally. She rarely expressed her true thoughts and feelings directly, and she often had to contain feelings of anger that either ate away at her or were displaced on her partner. At a much broader level, Marissa's colleagues were never challenged around their racial insensitivities because Marissa never dared to confront them. As a result, there was virtually no chance that her colleagues would develop racial awareness or sensitivity because Marissa did not call attention to their offenses. In fact, she became so good at playing along that a white colleague who was challenged by a black person in another department used Marissa as his "defense," claiming that she did not have the complaints that this other person was expressing. Marissa was angry when she learned about this, but said nothing directly to her colleague. Instead, she assumed a more indirect form of expression: she secretly talked with sympathetic colleagues and students about her colleague behind closed doors and, in so doing, she built a wave of negativity against him.

The Oppressed Oppressor Habit of Survival

Those with the **oppressed oppressor habit of survival** respond to oppression by identifying with the oppressor. Like those with the subservience habit, they internalize their oppression such that the rage and frustration associated with oppression are directed at the self. The key difference, however, is that those with the subservience habit channel their rage and frustration at their literal self, while those with the oppressed oppressor habit channel these emotions toward their symbolic self (e.g., other oppressed people). The organizing mental framework varies between the following: "I am not oppressed" and "Our suffering is our own fault and all we have to do is just pull ourselves up by the bootstraps." As a result, there are varying degrees of awareness among those with the oppressed oppressor habit in regard to being oppressed, but all who assume this habit share an underlying disdain and contempt for members of their own group.

The behavioral tendencies associated with the oppressed oppressor habit are:

- Assuming the characteristics of the oppressor (e.g., blaming the oppressed for their suffering; using tactics of domination to establish power over others, ruthlessly exploiting others to advance self-interest).
- Being skillful at ascending through the ranks of traditional institutions and organizations.
- Having self-hate that manifests through misplaced aggression toward their symbolic self (other oppressed people).
- Holding a generalized defensiveness and aggressiveness that usually represent an underlying fear and anxiety about being "discovered."

Perhaps the most functional aspect of the oppressed oppressor habit is the ability to advance through the ranks of traditional systems of power. Those who adopt this habit tend to achieve positions of leadership within mainstream institutions. Also, while it may seem counterintuitive, those with this habit also tend to harbor a strong sense of pride related to their group identity. However, that pride is deceptive because it is rigidly narrow and involves the complicated psychological processes of spite and projection.

Those with the oppressed oppressor habit take all of the traits associated with their group and split them into two categories: (1) those they accept and identify with, and (2) those they reject and project onto their symbolic self. The traits with which they identify are only those that hold positive connotations for them, and they regard these as the true markers of their group identity. The rejected traits are those viewed as negative because they make the group vulnerable to failure and predation. Whenever oppressed oppressors observe any of these "bad traits" reflected in members of their group, it incites rage and leads to aggression against those persons. This aggression is rooted in the belief that individuals who manifest negative traits are responsible for making the group as a whole weak. Oppressed oppressors are less likely to hold oppressors accountable and, instead, will blame members of their group who manifest "deviant" traits that place the group as a whole at risk of failure. This, of course, is the dysfunctional dimension of this habit of survival.

Marilyn was a female senior administrator who assumed an oppressed oppressor habit around gender. She identified with traits like strength and the ability to withstand hardship as a characteristic of women in whom she felt pride. Conversely, she responded negatively to qualities like nurturance and sensitivity because she thought these traits made women as a collective weak and ultimately responsible for their victimization by men. Marilyn split off these qualities, viewing them as not emblematic of the group, but only of some group members who were "bad apples." These women were the ones responsible for placing the group at risk by personifying traits that made them susceptible to, and even responsible for, being victimized. Consequently, Marilyn was aggressive toward female junior faculty she perceived in this manner, and she projected all of her internalized self-hatred at them.

David was in his second year on the tenure track, working in a social science department at a large research-intensive university. He was single, worked on campus from 9 to 5, and wore a suit on a daily basis. David was embedded in a divided department where there was longstanding and open hostility between quantitative researchers (the department majority) and qualitative researchers (the department minority). David was a quantitative researcher and had cast his lot decisively with the department majority. This often entailed disparaging qualitative research openly and aggressively, dismissing his qualitative colleagues' accomplishments, and generally participating in the divisive behavior that kept the department locked in conflict. David did participate in black faculty organizations and mentoring programs, but he regularly challenged assertions of racism as excuses for not getting work done. He viewed his participation in such venues as helping stagnant organizations to change their orientation and raise their standards.

When another department was poised to make a senior hire who was African American, the recruitment involved a spousal hire in David's department (a black female assistant professor). Several faculty asked David about his opinion of the candidate, who was a qualitative researcher. Even though the candidate had published more research than David, in higher-impact journals, David not only failed to support her but vehemently criticized the quality of her research. More importantly, he demeaned her as an individual in hallway conversations by telling his colleague that he had heard (from unnamed friends at her current institution) that "she was crazy" and they should "not go near her with a twenty-foot pole." During the candidate's campus visit, David was cold and told her directly how little he thought of her work. When it came time to vote on whether the candidate would become a member of their department, David voted no. After a negative tally, one of the faculty members recommended a courtesy appointment (0 percent appointment) given that the candidate was definitely coming to the university because of the spousal appointment, but David again voted no. Later asked why he would turn down a free line to the department, David argued that having black faculty who do not meet quality standards creates problems for black faculty who work hard to prove they deserve to be in the academy. In fact, he understood his no vote to be progressive and for the benefit of black faculty at the institution.

David's struggle was that he was disconnected from the community. He was alienated from most other black people because he disliked them and most disliked him. Although he was aligned with many of his white colleagues, he was only conditionally accepted by them. David's lack of meaningful connections with others fed his alienation and isolation. But David was largely unaware of his feelings because he buried them deep within. The only emotion he was aware of feeling was rage, and he harbored a lot of it. He was not blind to the racism of his white colleagues and it infuriated him, but he was quick to subvert this rage and redirect it toward other blacks; in particular, those who he saw as compromising "the advancement of the race." As a result, he also lacked a clear understanding of why and with whom he was angry.

The Culturally Split Habit of Survival

Those with the **culturally split habit of survival** adapt to the conditions of their oppression by splitting into two selves: the institutional self and the indigenous self. The organizing mental framework of this habit differs depending on which self is being referenced. The institutional self assumes a stance that can be summarized in the following way: "This is who I am when I am in the oppressor's presence [e.g., the system]. In this context, I embody the cultural orientation valued by the oppressor." The organizing mental framework for the indigenous self is: "This is who I am when I am in the presence of black people. In this context, I embody the values reflected in my cultural roots."

It is critical to emphasize that, in the case of the person with a culturally split habit, both selves are genuine. It is not the case that one self is more real than the other, or that one is the real self and the other is a false self. Rather both selves represent two well-developed, completely authentic, yet totally polarized, parts of the individual.

In those with the culturally split habit, the rage and frustration associated with oppression are expressed only by the indigenous self and, therefore, only in the company of their own group. It is only in this context that individuals with this habit allow themselves to feel the freedom to express emotions like rage and frustration. The behavioral tendencies associated with the culturally split habit are:

- In the university context, adopting thought patterns, gestures, mannerisms, language, and behaviors that match the expectations of the specific organizational context.
- In the indigenous context, adopting thought patterns, gestures, mannerisms, language, and behaviors that match expectations of the person's specific cultural context.
- Never revealing any aspects of the institutional self in the indigenous context or any aspects of the indigenous self in the institutional context.

The functional aspect of this habit is that individuals are able to adapt their behavior to fit the cultural demands of either context. Black faculty who adopt this habit are fully bicultural and therefore able to function seamlessly within both the institutional and indigenous contexts. The dysfunctional aspect of this habit is that these two selves are completely polarized so that the individual never feels the freedom to integrate these two separate identities. As a result, culturally split faculty members can suffer from a deep inner sense of disconnection, isolation, and loneliness.

Jack was a soon-to-be-tenured associate professor, a promotion he was to receive as part of a retention offer made by his university in order to fend off a more prestigious institution's efforts to recruit him. Jack grew up as the oldest of six siblings in a working-class family in

Philadelphia. He was an outstanding student who excelled at sports, and because of his cutting humor and verbal dexterity, he had a reputation for being a master at playing the dozens. Additionally, from an early age, Jack was passionate about racial justice. After he read *The Autobiography of Malcolm X* at the young age of twelve, he made so many references to the great leader that he became known among his family and friends as Jax (a contraction of Jack X).

Subsequent to earning his undergraduate degree, Jack went on to receive graduate degrees from top-ranked programs in his discipline. When he was ABD, he received a lucrative offer from a large research-intensive university, and he quickly became one of the most valued and respected junior faculty in his department. Jack was highly respected for his intellect, accomplishments, and drive. Although many of his senior white male colleagues resented what they perceived to be Jack's sense of entitlement, they nonetheless respected his achievements. Jack's few black colleagues admired the sense of power and authority that he commanded. They often said, "He expects to be treated like a white man!"

What is critical to understand about Jack is that he negotiated the dichotomy between African American cultural contexts and the expectations of mainstream social institutions by internalizing the divide. He had two distinct personalities living within one body. To his family, friends from home, and other nonacademic black people, he was Jax (his indigenous self). Among his academic colleagues, he was Jack, his institutional self. These two selves were each unique and distinct, and he never allowed crossover of the two.

When he was not in a professional context, Jax refrained from discussing his work life, preferring to downplay and deflect attention from his professional accomplishments. He therefore was often teased by his family and friends about being a "mystery man" because they knew that he was a university professor, made great money, and was highly accomplished, but they had little knowledge of his professional life beyond those basic facts. For a variety of reasons, they never sought more information and Jax did not offer anything unsolicited. Rather, his indigenous self was far more interested in spending time jesting with his brothers, engaging in loud heated debates about current issues in the black community, enjoying the music of his favorite rap artists, and playing with his nieces and nephews.

In contrast, Jack spoke perfect standard English, interacted with colleagues formally, and made a point not to run his schedule on "Colored People's Time" (CPT). Jack avoided any references to his favorite music or food preferences. Because he was all about business, he rarely if ever revealed any information about his personal life. In fact, most of his colleagues did not even know where he lived and had never met his partner. Jack remained intensely focused on his academic goals and pursued them with a fierce sense of purpose. As a teacher, he was beloved by his students. As a researcher, he experienced great success, including being the recipient of several large federal grants, and he published prolifically. Jack was viewed as a leader by his peers and was highly respected for his great intellect, masterful debating skills, and intellectual intensity.

The struggle that Jack faced was that he had so effectively divided his indigenous and institutional selves that he suffered from an internal divide that he once referred to as a "type of schizophrenia." Whether it was accurate or not, he believed wholeheartedly that neither of his two worlds could understand (much less accept) his other self. He believed that his family and friends would see his institutional self as "trying to be white" and as a "sellout." He believed that his colleagues would see his indigenous self as "too black," which in their view would mean too "loud," "emotional," and "unsophisticated." As a result, Jack kept his two selves divided and never allowed them to commingle. The price he paid was that he felt divided, which contributed to feelings of isolation and stress. Maintaining the divide was often exhausting and, many times, he felt burned out and drained by the effort it required.

How Habits of Survival Impact Promotion and Tenure

Without a doubt, some habits are better suited to pursuing advancement within academe than others. Each for different reasons, the subservience, feigned subservience, oppressed oppressor, and culturally split habits are all suited to succeeding within academic systems. And every one of these habits also breeds a corresponding set of challenges. In this section, we outline the respective challenges for those who have adopted each habit.

Those who have adopted a subservience habit are very likely to do well on their road to tenure to the extent that they will not threaten those in power and will work hard to placate the demands imposed on them by their more senior colleagues. The predictable challenges for black faculty members with this habit are that they can quickly become overworked, undervalued, and exploited. Agreeing to assume additional work assignments and being eager to excel at every task and demand can quickly lead to exhaustion and internal resentments that can gradually erode energy and emotional well-being.

Black faculty who adopt the feigned subservience habit also are likely to be successful in pursuing tenure and promotion because, on the surface, they appear to be as compliant and eager to please as those with the subservience habit. For this reason, they typically are well liked among their departmental colleagues. At the same time, because the underbelly of the feigned subservience habit is covert resistance, there is the ever-present risk of exposure. Should any of the power brokers within the system begin to suspect or obtain evidence revealing the hidden and less collegial agenda of those with the feigned subservience habit, this can create tension and generate barriers toward winning tenure.

Those with the oppressed oppressor habit also are highly likely to excel in their journey toward tenure by virtue of their strong identification with the system. Because they feel kinship with the system, there are no internal conflicts relative to their personal professional aspirations and the values of the system. Their identification with the system leads them to manifest one of the system's key values: the pursuit of power and a willingness to dominate others. Black faculty exhibiting this habit are strongly inclined to gain power and use it over others and, as such, are likely to be rewarded for their behavior. The challenges they are apt to face will be in relationships with others who experience oppression, especially members of their own group. Because of their aggression toward their symbolic self, they are prone to develop antagonistic relationships with other black people on campus who do not fit their narrow view of "the right way to be a black faculty member."

Culturally split black faculty members are extremely well positioned to excel within academe. Because they understand and can enact the attitudes and behaviors valued by the system, they are apt to be viewed as an "honorary member of the group" and rewarded for this. The challenge that is liable to arise, however, is that those who possess this habit will tend to feel inwardly disjointed and isolated. Over time, their dual existence arising from their polarized identities can become exhausting to maintain. In addition, the risk of having their other self revealed in the "wrong context" can generate feelings of intense anxiety accompanied by a sense of loneliness and a feeling of never quite belonging anywhere.

The warrior habit is the one habit of survival that is fundamentally ill suited to the process of pursuing tenure and promotion. Black faculty who have developed this habit personify behaviors that, more often than not, threaten and unnerve those in positions of power. They quickly become labeled as malcontents and troublemakers, and the system is oriented to weed them out long before they even make it to tenure review. In instances where those with the warrior habit get that far in the process, it is typically because they have been able to secure an ally among the power brokers or have amassed a commanding level of financial or political power (e.g., securing grants, achieving a high-profile public reputation) that leads the system to "tolerate" them.

Shifting from Habits of Survival to Strategies for Success

Black faculty at predominately white institutions are persistently faced with limited and narrow options that involve facing some form of negative outcome no matter what they do. This double bind is inherent to circumstances of oppression ("You're damned if you do and damned if you don't."). On one hand, you can choose to submit to subjugation and minimize being punished. But that submission can result in feeling as if you have sacrificed a piece of yourself. On the other hand, you can choose to push back and resist injustice. But while that resistance may allow you to retain your integrity and feel emotionally liberated, it can also lead to retaliation, punishment, or tenure denial. As a result, this no-win situation presents a set of "choices" that each entail some form of destruction.

Habits of survival have enabled oppressed people to endure and persist amidst horrific conditions and in the midst of the bind that oppression imposes. Ultimately, however, quality of life is defined by more than mere survival. A life worth living is characterized by *liberation*, and this requires having the ability to exercise conscious choices about your way of being in the world. The process of moving toward liberation involves replacing habits of survival with **strategies for success**. A *strategy* implies something that is deliberate, purposeful, conscious, and chosen. In other words, liberation involves shifting from being on "automatic pilot" to exercising "critical consciousness." It calls for a state of directed engagement with the realities of one's condition that are integrated with purposeful, intentional action in relationship to negotiating that condition.

Strategies for success do not involve transcending destruction because some form of destruction is inevitable when a person is oppressed. Rather, the critical difference is that, by employing strategies instead of habits, you can live through conscious, purposeful action that is designed to achieve some element of liberation rather than merely get by on automatic, habituated, and unconscious action that is designed to avoid some form of destruction. Shifting from habits of survival to strategies for success involves having an awareness of the dilemma that oppression imposes and making deliberate, intentional choices based on gaining something rather than avoiding something. Habits of survival are rooted to some extent in fear, reactivity, and avoidance, in effect saying, "I do _____ to avoid _____" (e.g., to avoid either spiritual or physical destruction). Alternatively, strategies for success are flexible, deliberate, and intentional proactive actions designed to acquire degrees of liberation. In other words, "I do _____ to gain _____" (e.g., to gain either spiritual or physical survival).

Shifting from habits of survival to strategies for success also involves selecting from a wide range of possible emotional and behavioral responses that can be applied to fit different contexts. For those who are oppressed, having the flexibility to draw from the cognitive, emotional, and behavioral characteristics of each of the habits is the essence of freedom, liberation, and health. For example, this means being able to consciously choose from all of the following options:

- Asserting, resisting, fighting.
- Taking a one-down position and being vulnerable.
- Working with and pushing against the system.
- Integrating pride and shame.
- Integrating the institutional and cultural selves.
- Acting on behalf of the liberation of your group.
- Understanding the complexity of your condition.
- Balancing physical and spiritual survival.

Going back to Marissa's case, after much focused effort, she had come to identify her habit of survival as feigned subservience, and she had examined the ways in which this habit had been both an asset and a liability throughout her life. Although she wished to retain the benefits from her habit, she wanted to minimize the liabilities and understood that this meant she would have to replace her habit of survival with strategies for success. She already had taken the first essential step by becoming conscious of her habit. Her consciousness was a start toward operating from a position of chosen actions rather than automatic and rigidified patterns of actions. With her newfound awareness, Marissa could make conscious, chosen, intentional choices about how to respond to situations in her life, which would mean that she was no longer driven and controlled by her habit.

The first major test of the shift from her habit of survival to strategies for success came when she was faced with a difficult relationship with the editor of her first book. Her former editor had left the publishing company and, as a result, Marissa found herself having to work with a new editor, Dan. Much to her dismay, Marissa found Dan to be noncollaborative, disrespectful, and disinterested in her views and ideas. He began their working relationship by informing her that he had read the first draft of her book and was going to e-mail specific directions about how she should begin making revisions. Marissa was immediately put off by the way that he spent so little time engaging with her on a more social and friendly level, which could have set the stage for a comfortable working relationship. She also was unhappy that, instead of consulting with her about the first draft and having a dialogue about his concerns, he merely told her what he expected her to change to accommodate his views. He did not solicit her opinions or even ask if she agreed with his opinions.

The final straw for Marissa came when it was time to settle on a title for the book and Dan informed her that the title she had worked with from the start would have to be replaced. He then offered three title options and told her to select one. Marissa was furious because none of the three appealed to her and truly reflected her work. It made her wonder how much Dan understood the point of her book. Moreover, she again resented his top-down approach, which consisted of telling her what to do rather than consulting with her about options and negotiating a final decision. She realized she needed to do something, but was unsure of what. The old Marissa, guided by the feigned subservience habit of survival, would have acquiesced to Dan even as she felt secretly resentful, which would have led her to find indirect ways to lash out against him.

In the spirit of challenging her habit of survival and shifting toward strategies for success, Marissa brainstormed how she could deal with Dan in a way that was more direct and honest, but that would minimize antagonism and reprisal. Eventually, she decided to call Dan and explain that she appreciated the energy he was devoting toward her book and valued his expertise about the publishing industry and marketing. At the same time, Marissa wanted to convey that she too had expertise to bring to the table (i.e., with regard to her subject matter) and was disappointed that, so far, he had made little effort to acknowledge it or to solicit and consider her views about issues affecting her book. In particular, she wished to voice strong disagreement with the book titles he was proposing as alternatives to her title. Despite the fact that she preferred her working title because she believed it most accurately reflected the point of her work, she was open to exploring other titles. She hoped that he would see the value in soliciting her opinions on this matter and in collaborating with her to make a final selection. She planned to conclude by saying that she realized he had ultimate authority over decisions pertaining to her book, but hoped that he would not overlook the wisdom and insights she had to offer with respect to these issues.

The outcome of Marissa's conversation with Dan is only marginally relevant here. Of far greater importance is the fact that she was able to operate from a position of consciousness by recognizing her habitual way of responding to similar situations and by opting to think through and make an informed, purposeful decision about how to respond this time. After weighing her options, Marissa opted to draw on a different set of skills than she had normally relied on. She decided to address Dan directly instead of silently acquiescing and covertly lashing out against him later. She realized that, in this situation, she had more to gain from being forthright. Not only would speaking directly leave her feeling better and more "whole," it also would make it possible for something to change in a positive way.

Hearing about Marissa's feelings would allow Dan to understand the impact of his approach on her and to choose to respond in a different and possibly more constructive way. Of course, he also could ignore Marissa's concerns or respond angrily. But if he moved in that direction, there was little more he could do to punish Marissa beyond what he had already done that was offensive to her. So she had nothing to lose, and everything to gain, by addressing Dan directly. In this way, Marissa was able to effectively shift from operating out of her habit of survival toward relying on strategies for success.

Personal Steps to Move Forward

The specific steps that any individual may take in shifting from habits of survival to strategies for success will vary depending on the habit in question. The following section lists several key actions that individuals can practice to begin transforming their habit of survival.

Subservience Habit
- Get clear about who the oppressor is in your context. Name those who are pressing down on you.
- Identify your needs and desires, first to yourself, and then gradually begin to assert your needs to others.
- Recognize when you are being pressed down on and make a conscious effort to resist by making your subjugation explicit and vocalizing your unwillingness to accept it.
- Channel your rage and frustration outward in constructive ways.

Warrior Habit
- Take time to focus on other pursuits and areas of your life in addition to your cause or mission.
- Consciously practice the art of relaxing.
- Explore your vulnerabilities and fears about risking intimacy and closeness with others. At the same time, gradually challenge yourself to take more risks in this regard.
- Recognize instances where it might be more effective for you not to resist and push back.
- Develop a set of criteria that will help you pick your battles.

Feigned Subservience Habit
- Identify instances where you can take calculated risks to push back against injustices in a direct way.
- Challenge yourself to be more trustworthy in close relationships.
- State directly what you want and need without manipulating others to get it.

Oppressed Oppressor Habit
- Get clear about who the oppressor is, and start holding oppressors directly accountable for their misuse of power.
- Integrate your cultural pride and shame to develop a more complex and expansive definition of being a member of your group.
- Examine how your identification with the system and aggression toward your symbolic self are a way of doing the oppressor's work for him or her.

Culturally Split Habit
- Move toward integrating your institutional self and your indigenous self.
- Try taking calculated risks to share parts of your institutional self in your home context.
- Try taking calculated risks to share parts of your indigenous self in your work context.

In addition to the specific tasks related to moving beyond your habit of survival, the process of shifting from habits of survival to strategies for success involves following several steps. Each of these steps is intended to help you identify your current habit of survival, become conscious of your behavior and assumptions, and transition toward a more expansive set of behavioral options in your professional life.

1. Identification. Identify your habit and how it organizes your thoughts, emotions, and behaviors on a regular basis. Before you can shift from habits of survival to strategies for success, you have to first know what your habit is. You must be aware of your orientation so that you can begin the process of replacing unconscious ways of thinking, behaving, and being with conscious, chosen, intentional ways. As you have read this chapter, you probably not only have identified your core habit of survival but also have come to better understand the habits of the people around you. It is also possible that you can recognize bits and pieces of yourself in each of the habits of survival, so try to identify the one that best characterizes your behavior.

2. Mindfulness. Consciousness is the antithesis of a habit of survival. Achieving consciousness is similar to the process of becoming mindful, which is a technique that involves observing your thoughts, feelings, and behaviors. It is a process of noticing what you are experiencing. To be mindful is to observe your own thoughts, feelings, and behaviors without judgment. Developing this sense of overt awareness about what you are thinking, feeling, and doing is a critical step toward being able to release or let go of cognitions, emotions, and actions that may be counterproductive. Becoming mindful allows you to loosen and let go of attachments to thoughts, feelings, and conditioned ways of behaving.

Focused breathing is often used as a means for helping to develop mindfulness, but we can learn to become mindful in less formal ways. You can bring your mind to focus on what is happening in the present moment in many different ways. Simply focusing on the sounds of rain hitting a rooftop or the sensation of the sun on your face or of the feelings in your body while stretching are ways of becoming mindful. Similarly, noticing your mind's usual commentary is a way of becoming mindful. Once you have noticed your mind's running commentary, you are free to release the judgments inherent in that commentary. For example, your mind is saying, "When I am criticized, I back down, so I'm a coward," you can elect to release the judgment and recognize that, when you are criticized, you back down. Getting criticized and backing down are nothing more than that. It is not necessary to judge the process, but only to be aware of what it is. Once this awareness is manifest, you have the opportunity to choose how you will behave.

Use mindfulness as a way to become aware of your habit of survival. Strive to become conscious of your habit, to recognize when it is activated, and to notice how it is compelling you to act. When you are able to do this, you will already be shifting away from habitual behavior. Although your conscious and chosen behaviors may mirror some of those that were part of your habit, the mere fact that your actions are deliberate choices means you are no longer stuck in habit mode.

3. The roots of your habit. Identify the conditions and dynamics you experienced in growing up that inclined you toward developing your particular habit of survival. What habits of survival did your primary caretakers embody and how did this affect you? Remember the case study of Sandra whose habit of survival was subservience. She learned this habit from her parents, in particular her mother. She observed her mother's subservience habit, which socialized Sandra to adopt a similar approach. Your family history can also work in the opposite way. For example, Sandra might have been so dismayed by her mother's subservience habit that she moved in the opposite direction by instead adopting a warrior habit. We make no claim that a particular childhood experience will render a particular outcome. We only argue that family history has some impact on the type of habit of survival that a person develops, and therefore, a critical part of shifting from habits of survival to strategies for success involves exploring your history. Recognizing the experiences that contributed to the formation of a particular habit will help you to take the steps necessary to shift from habits to strategies.

4. Gains and losses. Identify and celebrate the functional aspects of your habit. In other words, what benefits have you derived from using your habit of survival? Then, consider the dysfunctional aspects of your habit of survival. What losses or disadvantages have you suffered as a result of this habit? The point here is to embrace the fact that, as with everything in life, there are good and bad aspects to habits of survival. You developed your habit because it helped you to negotiate and endure difficult circumstances. Your habit was necessary, and it faithfully served you through challenging times. At the same time, you paid a price for your habit of survival. It stifled parts of you and kept you narrowly locked into a limited range of thoughts and actions. And depending on your particular habit, there also were other costs. For example, if you had a warrior habit, you most obviously gained satisfaction from speaking truth and pushing back against people and situations that otherwise would have silenced and bullied you. At the same time, you also likely suffered from limited connection and growth in intimate relationships. Whatever your habit of survival, you will have a list of resultant gains and losses, and we strongly recommend that you take the time to begin identifying your list and reflecting on it.

5. Alternative behaviors. Consider the specific behaviors you could engage in that are beyond the choices associated with your habit of survival. Try to consider the full range of possible responses for a particular situation. What anxieties and fears do you feel when you imagine your-self using these behaviors? What could you lose and what could you gain from using different behaviors?

Developing alternative ways of thinking and behaving is challeng-ing because it first requires you to push against the grain. The very na-ture of a habit is that it is automatic and rigidified. Hence, the prospect of entertaining alternative ways of being and doing means that you have to take yourself off autopilot and commit yourself to the work of being conscious and flexible. Much like working out your muscles for the first time, this work tends to be awkward and painful in the beginning, but over time it gradually becomes easier.

We encourage you to begin the process of exploring alternative be-haviors mentally. In other words, before you actually try to do some-thing differently, focus on mentally identifying what you might do in a given situation that is different from what you are oriented to do. In any given situation, imagine what it would be like to employ a behavior that is alternative to what your habit would guide you to do. What would it feel like to do something different, and what would happen as a result? Even if you do not do anything differently, think about what it would be like if you did. Being able to see alternatives in your mind, and to imag-ine what they would feel like, is the first step to actually acting in new, more expansive ways.

6. Exercising choice. In any given situation, before you do anything, stop to consider the situation and the options available for your response. Then, being fully aware that whatever you do (or do not do) is your choice, take the course of action you deem best. The key here is to be con-scious of your options, and to make a fully informed and intentional de-cision about how to respond. The course of action you ultimately employ in a given situation is less important than how you engage in this course. If you act unconsciously, without being mindful or aware of what you are doing and why, this means you are still on autopilot and your habit of sur-vival is in charge. However, if you are conscious of what is happening around you, aware of how you are feeling and the thoughts you are hav-ing, you will be able to consider different ways of responding, and exer-cise a conscious, purposeful choice about how you will behave. This is the essence of freedom and the purpose of the strategies for success.

Summary

Our basic premise in this book is that black faculty who work at pre-dominately white colleges and universities are embedded within institutions that are not constructed for their success, and yet they have to succeed anyway. In this chapter, we have attempted to make visible the invisible dilemma that black faculty face: having to choose between two forms of loss. On one hand, there is the threat of losing professional success (ultimately represented in the form of tenure) and, on the other hand, there is the threat of losing personal integrity (represented in the form of your soul). Although all junior faculty are faced with this dilemma to some degree, it is much more pronounced, intense, and complicated for black faculty. By virtue of their status as racial minorities, black faculty are confronted with systematic threats to their soul and survival.

We have argued that the development of habits of survival may have helped you to survive in your academic career, but that it is crucial to become conscious of your habits—and expand beyond them—in order to truly thrive in your institutional context. The nature of habits of survival is that they are neither conscious nor chosen. Instead, they are ways of being that individuals assume automatically as a way of negotiating and enduring in the face of oppressive conditions. Yet the very thing that makes habits helpful also makes them problematic: as automatic responses, they preclude conscious decisionmaking. And because the essence of liberation is the ability to make choices, we encourage you to spend time now (before moving on to the next chapter) to identify your habit of survival and consider how the strategies outlined to move forward may look in your individual life circumstances.

Note

1. The *habits of survival* were originally conceptualized by Tracey Laszloffy and presented as a workshop with Kenneth Hardy, "Habits of Survival: Family Therapy with Minorities," at the 51st annual conference of the American Association of Marriage and Family Therapists, Anaheim, California, October 1993.

9 | Constructive Conflicts

DEALING with conflict in the academy is at the heart of black faculty success and the maintenance of personal integrity. Consequently, this chapter is the heart of *The Black Academic's Guide to Winning Tenure—Without Losing Your Soul*. Everything we have outlined so far brings us to this moment. In previous chapters, we have elaborated on what most of you already learned through lived experiences: how racism shapes life for black faculty in colleges and universities. We have provided a set of necessary skills and techniques for strengthening your tenure case in terms of scholarship, teaching, and service, and for enhancing the fit between your institution and your system orientation. We also have discussed the unique issues that you bring to your situation by virtue of your habit of survival. All of this is critically important to moving forward in your academic career. But we now must get down to the key issue facing black academics—the issue that stands at the center of the struggle to win tenure without losing your soul—how to negotiate conflict constructively.

On a routine basis, you will face people and situations that challenge you. An opinion or policy may horrify you, or a particular comment, action or inaction, or circumstance may leave you feeling slighted, insulted, or offended. These disagreements, irritations, and offenses may or may not be racially based. Certainly, if there is an underlying racial dimension, the conflict becomes more "loaded." But even if the issue is not racial, you are vulnerable with regard to any conflict that arises by virtue of your position as a person of color within a predominately white institution. This is part of the dilemma of being black faculty on the tenure track. Do you dare to assert positions or share reactions that challenge those who are in positions of power over you?

Should you engage in conflict if it could negatively impact their assessments of your "collegiality" (and, by extension, your tenure case)? Does it make sense to avoid conflict if doing so could compromise your integrity and your soul?

It is critical to remember at all times that there are two important, yet often contradicting, goals to achieve and that you will have to find a way to be faithful to both. The first is that you have to **win tenure**, and the second is that you must **retain your soul** in the process. This requires knowing how to play the game by the **stated rules** (research, teaching, and service requirements). You will have to be exceptional at playing by the stated rules and fulfilling the system's explicit expectations of you. At the same time, a set of **unstated rules** also shapes your experience. The unstated rules, which are rooted in white supremacy, afford unfair opportunities to your white colleagues while imposing unfair constraints on you. In almost every way, the unstated rules will make it more difficult for you to fulfill the stated rules than your white junior colleagues. Nevertheless, these unstated rules cannot be allowed to prevent you from attaining success at your institution.

Importantly, whatever you do to win tenure, and however well you play by the stated rules, you will face insensitivities, indignities, and injustices along the way because of the unstated rules. Each and every time this happens, you will be challenged by the dilemma of whether to push back or pull back knowing that there will be costs associated with either choice. At times, it will be in your best interest to **pull back** and let something slide. But there will be even more times when you will need to **push back** because, if you do not, whatever is gained by hopefully securing tenure will be lost by virtue of compromising your soul. The "trick," so to speak, is to find ways to push back that allow retention of your integrity while minimizing retaliation from colleagues and administrators. This is what we mean by **constructive conflict**, and learning how to engage in it is the focus of this chapter.

What follows are two typical conflict scenarios that allow us to consider how to engage in constructive conflict. You may have met with something similar to one or both of these scenarios. In the first one, the faculty member had to decide whether or not to confront two colleagues with his concerns about their action and inaction during a faculty discussion of diversity in hiring. In the second scenario, the faculty member confronted her chair to challenge the outcome of her annual evaluation and now had to decide how she would negotiate the tension that had been made explicit between them. The scenarios are followed by a discussion of the elements of constructive conflict that will help you to recognize the unstated rules of engagement in your department, identify your own relationship with conflict, and then communicate clearly. After that, we return to the two scenarios to imagine how they might be resolved using the strategies we outline.

Scenario 1: Diversity and Future Hiring Priorities

Michael, a first-year faculty member in a professional school, was the only African American in a department where all of his colleagues were white and all but two were male. At a recent department meeting, the chair asked faculty to discuss the emphasis that they wanted to place on "diversity issues" in future hiring priorities. For a split second, Michael was relieved that someone other than himself had raised this issue for attention. But a moment later, he felt his heart sink when Frank, one of his senior white male colleagues, asked for the floor. Michael had avoided Frank both because their initial conversations were unpleasant and because he was unimpressed by Frank's proudly sexist comments and good ol' boy mentality. Given that Frank had voiced something offensive in each of their conversations, Michael was fairly certain that whatever Frank had to say probably would not sit well with him. His stomach tightened as Frank said:

> I hope we're going to place our emphasis on finding the candidates with the most impressive credentials and not get bogged down in being politically correct. Our only priority should be finding the most qualified candidate. If it so happens that the most qualified candidate is a minority, then that person will end up on our shortlist. We don't need to call attention to the diversity issue. I'm trusting that the best candidates emerge and it doesn't require making a big production out of the diversity angle. Making a big issue of diversity is just a waste of time and a mistake.

Michael's heartbeat accelerated because he passionately disagreed with Frank, but he also knew that Frank held a lot of power among the faculty and was an opinion leader. As a result, Michael was reluctant to go out on a limb and challenge his colleague without support. He waited in the hope that someone else, someone tenured, *anyone*, would articulate an alternative opinion. Out of the corner of his eye, Michael noticed Ned, a recently tenured professor, shifting in his seat uncomfortably and could feel his gaze on him. Michael wondered what Ned wanted from him. Most likely Ned was wondering if Michael had been offended by

Frank's comments, but what Michael wanted to know was if Ned himself had been offended. Michael had grown weary of white people who were racially righteous when a black person was watching them, but let that righteousness fly out the door when around only white people. He knew this happened because previous white allies had confirmed for him what he had always suspected.

While Michael was simultaneously pondering how to proceed and wondering about Ned, he was surprised when Denise, a tenured white faculty member, said:

> I understand what you're saying, Frank. I do think our most important priority has to be on finding the most qualified candidate. And I think that, as long as we make sure to announce the position in places where underrepresented candidates are most likely to hear about it, then we will have the best chance possible of gathering together a broad pool of strong candidates.

Michael could see that Denise was trying to softly push back with Frank. She did it without taking him on directly, but by making the point that some type of intentional action had to be taken to ensure a diverse pool of candidates. Michael agreed with Denise's underlying supposition, except he did not understand the meekness of her approach. What did she have to be afraid of? She was tenured. Why were none of his tenured colleagues more willing to challenge Frank's arrogance about minimizing the need to prioritize diversity and his flawed assumptions that the playing field was level and that quality and diversity are mutually exclusive?

After the meeting, Ned stopped by Michael's office to chat. Before long, Ned told Michael how offensive he found Frank in the meeting. He then quickly rationalized his silence by saying, "But what can you do? Frank's never going to see things differently. He's so old-school." Michael listened to Ned with amazement, feeling irritated that Ned had not said this publicly. He paused for a moment, then decided he did not care if he offended Ned, and had to speak his mind:

> I just have to tell you that I really resent that you didn't say any of this in the meeting. You know how I see this: you stay silent in meetings because you don't want to risk alienating your white friends and colleagues. You want to protect your privilege. Then, you come to me behind closed doors and want to suck up to me, hoping I will be dumb enough to not see this for what it is. If you want me to believe you are someone who cares about diversity, then you're gonna have to stand up for it publicly.

Looking stunned, Ned sat there for a moment and then said, "Well, that wasn't my intention. I wasn't trying to 'look good' in front of everyone else and I'm not trying now to look good to you. You are way off on this." With that, Ned walked angrily out of Michael's office.

Needless to say, Michael and Ned's interactions were tense from that point onward. Michael began to worry that Ned was dealing with the offense in his typical secretive way: by talking badly about Michael to others behind his back. Michael felt angry, frustrated, and alone. And because he was alone and seemed to lack meaningful allies, he felt extremely vulnerable. In short, if he confronted Frank, it would likely lead to an all-out conflict and he would make an enemy of some powerful colleague in the department. This was especially risky now that he had alienated Ned. Michael was not sure what to do. Speaking out only jeopardized his position, yet not speaking out was eating away at him.

Scenario 2: Contesting an Annual Review

Sheena was an African American faculty member in the natural sciences at a small liberal arts college, where she had recently received her third year review. Although the department had voted to renew Sheena's contract, her written review was short on praise, but long on areas where she had to improve and the consequences if she failed to do so. Sheena was surprised and disappointed by the dismal review and found it difficult to continue working on a daily basis among colleagues who had rarely spoken to her, much less given her any feedback during her first three years. Sheena's department chair, Stephen, called her in for a one-on-one meeting to discuss her progress and the third year review. He informed Sheena that, without at least four to six solid publications, she would not make it through her tenure review, which he emphasized was "right around the corner." Stephen also pointed out that Sheena had received poor student evaluations, and the committee held that as another mark against her. Although he promised to advocate for her, Stephen wanted Sheena's explicit assurance that she was going to "buckle down, get to work, and turn things around."

Sheena was furious when she left the meeting with Stephen because (1) he had failed to recognize that she had two articles under review and a third article had received a revise-and-resubmit (R-and-R) response; (2) he did not acknowledge the subtle racism that was working against her; and (3) he had elected to frame her struggles as nothing more than a personal failure on her part to "work hard," which she found deeply offensive. After debating all night about what to do, Sheena decided that she was already sinking and therefore had nothing to lose by being honest and direct with Stephen about her feelings. In an act of e-bravery, she sent the following e-mail message:

> I have thought a great deal since our meeting and there are several key points I need to address with you that I think are critical to my case and have been thus far overlooked.
>
> Regarding my publications, I am not only required to have two publications by this point, but the expectation is that they will be in the top journals. If you remember correctly, there were a year's worth of delays in setting up my lab that were due entirely to departmental problems. These internal issues, over which I had no control, cost me an entire year of productivity and yet they were not taken into consideration during my evaluation. The fact that I have two sole-authored articles under review and an R-and-R at the top journal in our discipline was also never mentioned in the review, leaving the erroneous impression that I have not been productive in my research while here.
>
> As for my teaching evaluations, if only there was solid research to prove what faculty of color already know for a fact: white students don't respect black profs as much as they do white profs. I am continually questioned, countered, and tested on factual information by white students who think they know more than me because they're white and I'm black. This semester alone, nine students in my intro class asked if I had a graduate degree and I just doubt that happens to my white male colleagues. You may even recall the student who complained to you about me, accusing me of not being fair in my grading. If there is one thing I am extremely sensitive to, it's issues of fairness. I strongly believe this student was just angry because he couldn't stand a black woman having power and authority over him.
>
> Finally, I am concerned and offended that you summed things up by saying that what needs to happen from this point onward is that I need to "buckle down and work hard." I think this is an example of the very racism I confront on a daily basis, but that most white people fail to recognize. I am just curious: what would lead you to see my work ethic as the defining issue in my productivity? In addition to already completing three publications while teaching new courses every semester for three years, what else should I be doing to convince you I am a hard worker? I assure you, I'm working hard, very hard. And in fact, I did not get this far without being a hard worker. Whatever struggles I am facing here, I can say with confidence that my work ethic is not a part of the problem.

After receiving Sheena's e-mail, Stephen responded back with the following:

> It is disappointing to me that you have elected to frame the issue here as racial and have even gone so far as to accuse me of being racist. I

think it is a cop-out to hang any of this on race. You knew all along we expect you to have at least two publications by your third year and, in three years, you have not published anything. I'm glad you completed three manuscripts, but the requirement is that they be published.

Furthermore, it's true that your lab was not completed in the time frame you desired; however, the delays have nothing to do with race. Yes, you are the only black faculty member in the department, and you did experience delays. But that does not mean that we somehow intentionally caused your delays because of racism.

Regarding your teaching evaluations, of course, student evaluations are hardly objective measures of a teacher's effectiveness, but I think it is in bad taste for you to make this all about race. I wish that, any time I had to face a negative student evaluation, I could write it off as racism or sexism. I don't have that luxury. Instead, I just have to accept that there is something about me as a teacher that doesn't work for my students, right or wrong, fair or unfair. Might a particular student have some personal issue with you? Sure, this is possible, but you are trying to build a case for all-out racial bias on behalf of the students in your class.

I also want to say that I know you are a hard worker, and you have had many demands placed on you with new courses to prepare for and teach every semester. But you are not alone in this regard. We place a heavy demand on all junior faculty and, while it may be unfair, it is not unfair based on race. We don't only place these burdens on black faculty. Your white colleagues on the road to tenure have the same demands to negotiate.

Finally, I am offended that you would think my comments about working hard were racist. I don't see the connection here at all. I made this comment because I was trying to empower you . . . so you would see that you have the power to do what is needed to get tenure, and I was expressing faith and confidence in you and your abilities.

A mix of emotions overcame Sheena after reading Stephen's e-mail response. She was angry that he did not understand the racial aspects of her situation. She was fearful that she was now at greater risk because Stephen was offended and insulted by her e-mail. She was confused about how to proceed from this point. Sheena's anger made her want to escalate the conflict with Stephen. She wanted to deconstruct each of his comments and "make" him see how racially clueless, insensitive, and misinformed he really was. But her fear made her want to back away and retreat. After all, Stephen might want to let things slide out of a concern that any punishing actions toward Sheena might confirm her charge of his racism, which seemed to disturb him. Sheena was not sure what to do. Should she pursue things further in the hope of working things through, but with the risk of making them worse? Or should she let things cool down, even though it was eating away at her?

Black junior faculty encounter some variation of these two scenarios on a routine basis. At the heart of each scenario is a conflict and, in these cases, the conflicts have a decidedly racial dimension. The question is: how can black faculty in vulnerable positions negotiate conflicts like these in ways that will allow them to maintain some integrity?

Elements of Effective Conflict Resolution

How do you address conflict? As we consider the principles and strategies that will allow you to negotiate and resolve conflicts without losing your soul or jeopardizing your tenure case, we encourage you to think about recent conflicts in your department and how they might have been resolved differently.

Understand What Differentiates Healthy from Unhealthy Conflict

Before you can embark on the road to negotiating differences in constructive ways, you will first need to understand what differentiates healthy conflict from that which is unhealthy. **Conflict** is a natural part of the human experience. Whenever two or more people have differing views of reality (which is virtually all the time), conflict is likely to occur. In some cases, parties agree to disagree about their differences, thereby allowing for the peaceful coexistence of difference and avoidance of conflict. More often than not, however, when people have different views, tension and conflict arise as each party jockeys on behalf of their position. More important than *if* a conflict exists is *how* the parties involved handle and negotiate that conflict. In and of itself, conflict is not harmful. But conflict can become harmful when it is expressed in destructive ways or when one or more people attempt to use power to leverage their position so they can force the other to concede to their point of view, or punish them if they refuse.

Unhealthy conflict is based on a belief that it is necessary to change the other party. Both parties are unable or unwilling to accept the differences that exist. The orientation therefore is toward domination rather than pluralism, based on the assumption that there is a right and a wrong and it happens to be that "I am right and you are wrong." Unhealthy conflict also occurs when there is friction between people and the positions they hold. As a result, the conflict is not merely a matter of different ideas, opinions, beliefs, or ideologies, but it gets personal such that the positions and the personhood of the parties involved become indistinguishable. Finally, unhealthy conflict occurs when the strategies that are used to express conflict are aggressive. Whether verbal or physical, parties resort to attacking and wounding each other in an effort to see their position prevail. By understanding what distinguishes healthy from unhealthy conflict, you will be better able to resolve conflicts effectively.

Healthy conflict occurs when the parties involved accept each other's basic right to have their own position. At the same time that both parties believe passionately in their own perspective, they recognize that there are other ways of viewing reality and accept the right of others to hold their own views. This reflects a pluralistic orientation. Healthy conflict requires people to distinguish between positions and personalities, such that it remains possible to disagree vehemently with a position while still embracing the person who holds the position. As a logical extension of this, the strategies that are used during healthy conflict are never aggressive or dehumanizing, but instead can be passionate, intense, strident, and relentless in attacking a position without attacking the person who represents that position. When parties can clearly separate the person from his or her position, they are engaging in healthy conflict.

Know Your System's Conflict Rules

Within your institutional context, it is inevitable that conflict will arise. But every system has its own particular rules around conflict. The nature of the rules in your system will weigh heavily in how you can manage and resolve conflict.

Most academic institutions highly value **intellectual conflict**. Academics are known for their love of debating theories, methodologies, and research findings. Yet as much as academe encourages intellectual conflict, the implicit rules of most colleges and universities discourage open and direct **interpersonal conflict**. Although most academic systems have well-developed rhetoric affirming the importance of respecting differences and allowing for the free expression of multiple views of reality, this is not the way that most institutions function on a human, social, and emotional level. In fact, there are many examples of typical academic procedures that discourage open expressions of differences and disagreement. For example, tenure review committees are closed to non-tenured faculty, and there is neither a record of the discussion that occurs nor a list of members who vote for or against tenure. These critical discussions occur in private and nobody is accountable for his comments, positions, or vote. When the person being reviewed is informed about the decision, the conversation is defined as an "evaluation" whereby he is told the oucome of the vote, but in ways that do not invite a dialogue or encourage disagreement. Moreover, the identities and individual votes remain hidden so the recipient of the decision is powerless to hold the evaluators accountable. A similar process occurs when journal articles, research presentations, and grant proposals are submitted for consideration. Through a blind peer review process, those who provide critiques do so incognito where they are free to render any criticism without ever having to own up to it or be held accountable for their position. Processes like these are commonplace in academe and unfortunately they contribute to indirectness and secrecy that make it difficult for conflicts to emerge openly and to be addressed and resolved directly.

Although academe in general tends to subvert open, direct conflict, it is important to bear in mind that each academic system is unique and varies with respect to the rules that shape how conflict is expressed and negotiated. Therefore, you will need to survey your institution's system to assess its rules. Specifically, you must closely observe your institution's system to evaluate whether or not it is conflict tolerant or conflict avoidant.

In **conflict-tolerant institutional systems**, differences between people can be expressed overtly and parties are able to use direct strategies to assert their respective positions. In **conflict-avoidant institutional systems**, differences between people and the tension these create are pushed beneath the surface. In other words, conflicts are handled covertly. People may engage in strategies to advance their positions, but these strategies are hidden and indirect. For example, a party may quietly seek out another who will agree with her position to meet "behind closed doors" to gossip and complain about the person with whom her conflict exists. In conflict-avoidant systems, when someone dares to name a conflict overtly, more often than not others will altogether deny the conflict in an effort to keep it indirect and under the surface.

One of the key factors that shapes an institutional system's openness to conflict has to do with its tolerance for multiple views of reality. In systems where the view of those with the most power must prevail, open and direct conflict is strongly discouraged. In systems where multiple views of reality are genuinely tolerated, open and direct conflict is both expected and encouraged.

Recognize Your Relationship with Conflict

It is equally important to be aware of the relationship that you have with conflict. How comfortable are you with conflict, and how do you normally handle conflict? We all possess varying levels of comfort with and ways of handling conflict. Much of what you learned about conflict and how to engage in it occurred in your family of origin. The system in which you were raised prepared you to perceive and react to conflict in particular ways, which is one reason why it is useful to understand your familial roots and how these affected you, as we explained in Chapter 3. The system used in your family of origin and the system orientation you accordingly developed shape your relationship with conflict and will influence how you are inclined to handle conflict in your job.

It may be that you will benefit from seeking professional support to help explore your relationship with conflict and to resolve some of the deeper, underlying issues that interfere with your ability to conduct conflict in constructive ways. If, for example, you notice that you are consistently undermined by strong emotional reactions when you try to use the concrete strategies and techniques associated with effective communication (presented later in this chapter), it is a clue that you may have some issues to work through. This is where therapy can be valuable. Therapy offers the context and tools to help you identify and resolve any number of emotional blocks that may affect your conflict management competency.

Use Effective Communication Strategies

The ability to resolve conflicts constructively relies on the use of effective **communication strategies**. If the parties who are involved in a conflict fail to communicate in effective ways, conflict resolution is highly unlikely. What follows is a set of basic communication strategies to use as guidelines for constructive conflict. They will be especially helpful to you during attempts to address and negotiate conflicts in your department.

1. Be clear about your goals. Before you can effectively negotiate a conflict, it is imperative to be clear about what you hope to ultimately achieve. As a junior faculty member who is experiencing either **covert or overt conflict** with someone in your system, your goals will loosely fall into one of two categories. The first involves a need to influence a policy or course of action. For example, in the conflict scenario involving Michael, his goal was to make diversity a hiring priority. With this type of goal, a specific tangible outcome is sought. Communication and efforts at conflict resolution are focused on achieving the tangible outcome that is desired.

The second type of goal involves expressing beliefs, opinions, and feelings. This goal tends to arise when someone says or does (or fails to say or do) something that you disagree with and perhaps offends or hurts you. When this occurs, the goal is to express yourself, to go on the record asserting your disagreement or offense. It is critical to make clear that this goal is different from changing another person's position, attitudes, or behaviors. You *cannot* change anyone else. For example, you cannot change the view of an individual who harbors some racial prejudice that you find insulting. You can express disagreement and even convey how it makes you feel, but you cannot control anyone else's thoughts and behaviors. The most you can do is take responsibility for your position. In such cases, the goal is to nurture your integrity and spirit by voicing your truth, with the understanding that it probably will not change anything for anyone else, and that is okay.

2. Make power differentials overt. If you are in a one-down position, making explicit the implicit **power differential** is one way of disarming the more powerful party. After openly naming the power differential that exists, acknowledge that it is now risky for you to openly disagree or challenge from your one-down position. Acknowledge your reticence and vulnerability, and then clarify that the only reason you are going to take this risk is that you have some confidence in the other party's character. Explain that you trust that the other person values honesty and directness and is strong enough to deal with disagreements. All of this is a way of setting the other party up to be open and receptive to your disagreements because, whether he wants to or not, he will have to confirm that he is in fact strong enough and big enough to tolerate your disagreements.

3. Use "I" messages (not "you" messages) to claim your position. When you assert your position, it is crucial that you do so using **I messages** rather than **you messages.** Using you messages blames the other person and invites defensiveness. In contrast, when utilizing I messages, we take responsibility for our position and avoid the trap of attacking or indicting the other person. An I message cannot be challenged. If you say, "You were offensive," the other person can dispute that assertion, arguing that her behavior was not offensive. But if you say, "I was offended," this cannot be disputed. She cannot tell you what you did or did not feel. As a result, the most effective way to articulate your position is to use I messages.

4. Validate. As simple as it may seem, affirming the good in others goes a long way toward resolving conflicts. All of us want to feel recognized for the things about us that are positive, and, when this happens, it makes us more receptive to hearing things that may be harder to swallow. By affirming something that we value in the other person's character or position, we facilitate positive engagement. It is important to clarify that validating does not mean abandoning or weakening the basis for our conflict. Rather, it is completely possible to affirm something good about the other person while still arguing passionately about divergent views or positions. **Validating** humanizes the interaction and conveys the message that, as intense as a conflict may be, the parties involved are still able to exhibit basic respect toward each other at the end of the day.

5. Find common ground. Whatever the differences are between parties, there is always something that is shared by both. This **common ground** can be a value, goal, or experience. Identifying and highlighting whatever common ground exists between those who are in the midst of a conflict will form a bridge. Conflict resolution is possible only when each party gets some of what he needs, and often the easiest way to make that happen is by building on a point of commonality.

6. Employ strategic apologizing. **Strategic apologizing** for hurting someone is powerful and goes a long way toward enticing others to resolve things with you. Apologies are issued from a place of personal power. It takes personal power to be able to say, "I'm sorry." We strongly advocate apologizing when you hurt someone. And we make a critical distinction between apologizing for hurting someone and apologizing for your position. We advocate the former and not the latter in most cases. It is one thing to say, "I am sorry that I hurt you by taking that position" or "I am sorry that the way I expressed my position was hurtful," but something else altogether to say, "I am sorry for my position."

7. State what you want. For healthy conflict resolution to occur, both you and the other party must know what you hope to achieve and **state what you want** before you can feel resolved. This aligns with the first step in this process, "Be clear about your goals." First, you have to know what you want and need. Then, at some point in the communication process, you have to explicitly let the other person know what you want and need. It is helpful to be as specific as possible about your desired outcome in order to bring about a resolution.

8. Clarify message sent versus message received. Each party must reflect back on what she believes the other communicated. Asking the other person to feed back what she thinks you said provides the opportunity for you to clarify any misunderstanding. This is a way of ensuring consistency between the **message sent** and the **message received**. Additionally, when someone accurately feeds back what you said, or vice versa, it is validating because it helps us to feel heard.

9. Be aware of personal triggers and redirect emotional reactivity. We all have **personal triggers** that activate our **emotional reactivity** and, when this occurs, it throws us off balance. During conflicts, we are especially prone to having our emotional reactivity triggered. Reactivity distorts our perceptions and compromises our ability to see a situation clearly. While we are reactive, we are not in control of ourselves. Reactivity means that something external has activated a vulnerable spot within us, which then provokes us in some way that is beyond our control. When our reactivity is triggered, it is almost impossible to be emotionally composed and clear, making healthy communication unlikely. By knowing your triggers, you will be better able to recognize when you are about to become reactive and can adjust by pulling back and regaining your composure.

10. Attend to both the content and relationship levels of communication. Communication occurs at two levels. At the **content level of communication**, there is the substance of the words that we convey. Aside from the content that is exchanged, at the **relationship level of communication**, we are communicating about the nature of our association.

Consider the following example. Dalia was a junior faculty member approached by a senior colleague, Greg, to do a personal favor for him at the last minute. Dalia politely declined because she had an important previously scheduled meeting with a book editor who was considering publishing her first book. Greg responded by telling her, "I really like you, Dalia, so let me give you some advice. You need to stop acting like a graduate student and remember that service is an important factor in your tenure decision." Dalia responded by thanking him for his concern about her welfare and reiterating that she could not fulfill his request. In this example, the content of Greg's communication consisted of telling Dalia that he liked her and was trying to be helpful by warning her of the dangers of acting like a graduate student. But, at the relationship level, Greg was communicating that he had little regard for Dahlia's welfare, that he did in fact see her as little more than a graduate student, and that he was going to use his power to threaten her. In terms of Dalia's communication, her content conveyed that her preexisting commitment was important to her and that she appreciated his concern for her welfare. At the relationship level, however, she communicated that she saw herself as an equal and refused to allow herself to be intimidated by his power play.

Effective communicators are tuned in to both levels of communication and use their observations of what is being communicated at the relationship level to facilitate conflict resolution. They do this by making the relationship-level communication explicit. It is at this level that the "real" issues are acted out, and only by naming these does the opportunity to genuinely move forward exist.

Conflict Scenarios Revisited

At the beginning of the chapter, we introduced two common conflict scenarios. Each one ended with the junior faculty member in question wondering how to proceed in light of the existing conflict. In Michael's scenario, he had expressed disagreement with and anger toward a senior colleague, and found himself wondering (1) should I voice my position to the other colleague (Frank)? And, (2) if so, how? In Sheena's scenario, she had already expressed her disagreement with the department chair (Stephen) and he had pushed right back, making their conflict explicit and out in the open. Sheena's question was how to proceed in light of the fact that there was more she wanted to disagree with Stephen about, but she also was worried about negative consequences given his power over her in the system. In the following section, we provide a possible way for Michael and for Sheena to respond in the spirit of staying true to themselves while also taking steps to resolve their conflicts in a healthy way.

Michael

Michael's first task will be to set up a meeting with his colleague (Frank) so that he can express his concerns and disagreements. In his meeting with Frank, we would encourage Michael to say something like the following:

> I want to start by saying that I feel somewhat uncomfortable having this conversation with you because, of course, you have more power in the system than I do. And, in fact, you have power over me. So I'm in a vulnerable position. Some would say I should not take the risk of coming in here to share my disagreements with you [**naming unequal power**]. However, I want to believe that this is the type of place and you are the type of person that can tolerate open expressions of difference [**validating**]. I know that we have very different views about a lot of things, but I hope we can respect each other enough that we can be honest and direct without having this spiral into attacks and personal slights [**making the power differential explicit**]. That's my hope anyway.
>
> I want to talk with you about something that happened during our last faculty meeting that is still troubling me. I agree with you about

the importance of finding the most qualified candidates and I share and appreciate your commitment to excellence [**highlighting commonality**]. At the same time, I also think it is critical that we remain actively devoted to seeking out and finding candidates from underrepresented groups. I struggle with the point you made that, if we just look for the best candidate and there are any exceptional minorities, we'll just find that person [**I messages**]. That assumes that the playing field is level, which it never was and it still isn't. If we care at all about finding qualified candidates who are minorities, this will require active, intentional work on our part. I want us to include diversity in our hiring priorities so we have the foundation to then take targeted actions that will help us locate some of the best candidates who might not otherwise surface without these actions on our part [**stating wants or needs**].

Irrespective of how Frank responds to this disclosure, it will be important for Michael to reflect back on what Frank says and to ask Frank to do the same. Michael also will need to monitor his personal triggers and ensuing reactivity and, if he feels these are being activated, withdraw from the interaction until he can gain his composure. Michael also should stay attuned to the relationship level of communication because this is where he will have his most powerful feedback about where things stand between him and Frank.

Sheena

Because Sheena is in a different type of conflict situation with Stephen (her chair), she might consider the following face-to-face conversation:

I am feeling a little vulnerable now because you seem offended, and the reason that causes me a little anxiety is that we are not on equal ground. As the chair of this department, you have power over me so it feels uncomfortable knowing that you took such offense at my honesty [**naming unequal power**]. I would like to believe that this will be okay, that you want your faculty to be honest with you even when you don't like what they have to say [**validating**]. Having said this, I do want to clarify some things I said and address some of your reactions. I believe you have been supportive of me so far and I appreciate that. I think your intentions with me have been honorable and I want to acknowledge that from the outset [**validating**].
I feel very misunderstood about my racial concerns [**I messages**]. I hear you saying it's a cop-out to claim that race is related to some of my challenges here. Ironically, though, when you deny the racial issues, you're making my case. It's this type of unawareness on the part of white people that makes it easy for subtle racial insensitivities and biases to occur. It feels alienating to me that, as my chair, you do not see or acknowledge the ways that race unequally shapes experiences

between white and black faculty. It makes me feel like you don't understand something that is a fundamental and critical part of my professional experience. It would help me if you at least acknowledged that there is racial bias and that it subtly shapes things that happen, even in places like higher education, and as a result racial minorities face additional challenges that whites don't face. Acknowledging this would be a helpful starting point between us. We might disagree about the particular ways race is or is not affecting things for me in this department, but it would be meaningful to me if you would recognize that racial bias in higher education does exist [**proposing a common ground**].

I want to be able to work through our conflict here. That's important to me. I wasn't trying to attack you and, if I came off that way I am sorry [**strategic apology**]. At the same time, I feel totally misunderstood and invalidated around a number of things that are very important to me. I realize that we may never agree in the end, but I'd nonetheless like the opportunity to discuss these points in greater detail with you. Toward that end, it would help me if we could start with an explicit understanding that there is racial bias in higher education [**stating wants or needs**].

What is important about Sheena's communication to her department chair is that she apologizes if she hurt his feelings, she validates his positive intentions and support, and she retains her position. She also asserts her vantage point using I messages while providing a specific way the two of them can move toward a common ground as a starting point. She is not asking him to give up his position, but rather to expand it to leave room for the possibility of hers. She follows up by making a request for further dialogue rooted in this proposed common starting point. However her chair responds, she is doing what she can to exhibit respect for his humanity and to meet him halfway while not relinquishing her position or her needs.

Dangers of Avoiding (and Engaging in) Conflict

When you elect to sidestep the conflict that might arise by acknowledging and addressing an incident that you find offensive, the anger that you feel in the moment gets suppressed and buried. **Anger** is an instant emotional response to a perceived irritation or offense. If we express anger immediately, it is released and the energy associated with this emotion dissipates. On the other hand, because anger involves a form of energy, if we fail to release it when it arises and instead push it down and store it away, it grows, deepens, and expands to ultimately transform into rage. In contrast to anger, **rage** is a more intense and sustained emotion that takes root in the soil where anger has been buried over time.

If rage is suppressed and buried, it eventually will find its release in unhealthy ways. It may seek to escape by devouring its way out. Like a corrosive chemical, rage can eat away at your insides, causing physical symptoms ranging from depression to high blood pressure to digestive problems. Rage may also find its escape through exploding into an eruption. When this occurs, there often is an enormous gap between the issue in the moment that was the trigger and the intensity and aggressiveness of the resulting explosion. As a result, what onlookers see is someone whose emotional response seems inappropriately disproportionate to the presumed trigger. Of course, most onlookers do not know, and even you may not realize, that the emotion being expressed in the moment is actually the cumulative product of many prior incidents where anger and rage were buried rather than released.

Although there may be good reasons to avoid engaging in certain conflicts, or to elect not to directly express anger or rage in a given moment, avoidance and suppression as a general approach are dangerous. They place undue stress on the mind and body that can result in serious physical and mental illness. They also create vulnerability to an explosive outburst that can have a deleterious impact on interpersonal relationships. Displays of anger may be awkward, but they are far more socially tolerable than expressions of rage. Most people fear rage because it hints at violence. Therefore, when we observe someone who is enraged, it leaves a lasting and alienating impression.

The issue of anger and rage is especially complicated when we factor in race. Virtually all African Americans, as members of a racially oppressed minority, experience rage in response to racial injustice. Because racism is a persistent and pervasive reality for racial minorities, black people (and all people of color) are faced with an unending stream of assaults, which in turn contribute to a cauldron of rage. The rage that racism provokes is a normal healthy response to pain and injustice. However, because of the dynamics of racism, black people have limited opportunities to express rage without facing punishment. In other words, whenever black people seek to express normal, healthy responses to degradation and discrimination (which means rage), the system of power seeks to control them and keep them "in their place." The system does this by discrediting their feelings, delegitimizing their rage, and labeling them as "crazy," "dangerous," "emotional," "out of control," "unprofessional," and "irrationally angry." Certainly, these same dynamics are at play within academic contexts.

All junior faculty struggle to some extent with the issue of when and how to engage in conflict and express normal feelings of anger or even rage, but this struggle is far greater for black faculty. As black people positioned within a white supremacist environment, any expressions of irritation, anger, and rage—while completely justified and reasonable—will be "colored" by the politics of race. This is the challenge black faculty face at all times. Avoiding conflict and burying anger and rage are problematic. Yet it is a reality that, when black faculty attempt to engage in conflict and express normal feelings of anger and rage, they are more likely to be pathologized and punished than their white counterparts.

In our experience, we believe that the first thing to do is recognize and become internally clear about the issues and dynamics that exist. Second, it is critical to understand that, even though it may be tempting to avoid conflict and expressions of anger and rage, in reality this is a "solution" that rarely if ever can lead to a winning outcome. In the long term, avoiding conflict and suppressing anger and rage only place you more at risk. Therefore, it is critical to find ways to strategically pursue some issues while avoiding others, and to allow for periodic releases of emotion. An important strategy is to acknowledge anger and rage and address conflicts directly before they morph into corrosive energy that eats away at you from the inside or into a full-blown explosion directed at others.

It bears repeating that most black people, by virtue of living in a white supremacist society and working in predominantly white institutions, will always have to manage some level of racially based rage underpinning interactions and conflicts with white colleagues. This rage is valid, and it is important to recognize its presence and validate its existence. At the same time, it is critical to find ways to use your rage as a source of strength, to master it before it masters you. For example, artistic endeavors, sports, and social activism are vehicles for constructively channeling rage. The point is simple: you do not always have to release your emotion in the moment or in direct response to a particular trigger, but it is essential to find a vehicle for emotional channeling.

Deciding When to Push Back Versus When to Pull Back

Although it is important to be able to directly address differences and disagreements and to work through conflicts in healthy ways, the reality is that you cannot and should not take on every issue. There are occasions when it is best to simply let things slide. You have likely heard the common advice to "pick your battles." The trick is figuring out when to push back and when to pull back. We suggest pulling back if (1) the conflict is more about you than the other person, and (2) the issue at hand feels minor.

When It Is More About You Than the Other Person

There are some situations where the conflict you experience with someone else is really more about you than about the other person. For example, during a session with her therapist, Jennifer explained how irritated she was with one of her colleagues, Paul. She described him as a "kiss ass" who was always using abject flattery in an attempt to win people's approval. Jennifer was disgusted by his behavior, and told her therapist that she could barely be civil with him. In the spirit of addressing conflicts directly, which Jennifer had been working on in therapy, she wondered if she should confront Paul and tell him how aggravating she found his constant attempts to solicit her approval as well as that of others.

After listening to Jennifer's account of the situation, her therapist asked what Jennifer hoped to gain from confronting Paul. On closer scrutiny, Jennifer realized that, although it might feel good to confront him, she had no reason beyond that for doing so. Her motive was simply to "set him straight," not to resolve a specific conflict. She also realized that most of her reactivity toward Paul's disposition was about her own internal struggle with the part of herself that was similar to Paul. Prior to beginning therapy, Jennifer was more likely to avoid confrontations with others and, like Paul, she often went out of her way to win others' approval. She had come a long way through her therapy work, but a part of Jennifer would continue to fear the dislike of others and tempt her to sell herself out in the spirit of being "likable." Jennifer's discomfort with this part of herself was at the root of why she was so reactive to Paul. In essence, she wanted to attack Paul because of her desire to attack the part of herself that he represented. Realizing this, it became clear to Jennifer that her conflict with Paul was less about him and more about herself, and thus she had little to gain from confronting him.

It is important to point out here that Jennifer's ability to recognize the root of her reactivity to Paul and how it was getting in her way was greatly facilitated by her participation in therapy. There are tremendous benefits to be gained from entering into a therapy process with a skilled professional. We cannot overstate the progress junior faculty make in a solid relationship with a good therapist. The example of Jennifer is but one illustration of how useful therapy can be in working through the emotional foundation that can underlie conflict. We suggest that you begin interviewing therapists if you have never had a sustained and helpful therapeutic relationship or if you do not already have a trusted therapist.

Choose Your Battles

Inevitably, any number of issues will arise between you and your colleagues and between you and your institution. Taking them all on is unreasonable. Not only would a constant conflict engagement mode exhaust and burn you out, but it also would undermine your efficacy with others. Those who take on every issue are quickly discredited as troublemakers. Therefore, it is important that you critically examine the issues in which you are going to engage. In this exercise, it is best to focus on larger issues while letting smaller ones go. You might ask yourself the following types of questions to determine whether or not a given conflict situation is worth engaging:

- If I *take on this issue*, what are the *immediate* gains and losses to me and how will these likely impact my success at this institution and in my life overall?
- If I *take a pass on this*, what are the *immediate* gains and losses to me and how will these likely impact my success at this institution and in my life overall?
- What are the *longer-term* gains and losses to me if I *take on this issue* and how will these likely impact my overall success at this institution and in my life overall?
- What are the *longer-term* gains and losses to me if I *take a pass on this issue* and how are these likely to impact my overall success at this institution and in my life overall?

We asked you to consider the implications of each course of action in terms of success both in your institution and in your life overall because we want you to keep the larger picture in perspective at all times. If this analysis reveals that you have more to lose than gain, or your gains are probably going to be negligible, or your losses from doing nothing are going to be relatively minor, the issue is almost certainly one that you should let go of. But you may conclude that the gains from letting something slide in your workplace will come at too high a price in terms of your personal relationships, mental or physical health, spiritual contentment, and so forth. These also are factors to keep in mind when you weigh the costs and benefits of taking a particular course of action.

Beware of E-Bravery

E-bravery is the confidence and boldness that we manifest during electronic communication. There is something about staring at a blank and motionless screen that can imbue us with a sense of courage that is harder to access during face-to-face encounters. E-bravery consists of our willingness to risk direct and potentially offensive communication because we do not have to see the visceral impact of what we are saying on the other person. E-bravery also protects us from the vulnerability we feel during face-to-face encounters when we find ourselves reacting to and emotionally affected by the intensity of the interaction. Electronic communication also makes us e-brave because it allows us to "pause" interactions long enough to take the time we need to decide how we want to respond. During face-to-face communications, we are under pressure to respond "in the moment" in real time. Electronic communication gives those of us who are not quick on our feet the time to calculate our response.

The courage generated by electronic communication is positive to the extent that it enables us to communicate more clearly, honestly, and directly than we would otherwise dare to communicate in person. E-bravery is beneficial to the extent that it helps us to say things that we otherwise would not say. The problem is that it tends to create a false sense of security and power, which seduces many of us into expressing ourselves in unhealthy ways. Imagine, for example, that you are frustrated with a colleague who sits with you on a university committee and has consistently failed to follow through on commitments in a reliable way. Imagine also that you are conflict avoidant and prefer to sidestep direct communication in favor of suffering in silence. Yet you realize that, if you do not address these concerns with the colleague, nothing is going to change. Therefore, you decide to e-mail the colleague because the safety associated with electronic communication gives you the courage to confront her. In fact, the sense of safety and power from hiding behind the computer screen lead you to bypass the effort to craft your communication with diplomacy. As a result, you are honest about your irritation (which is positive), but the way that you express yourself is attacking and alienating (which is negative). Though the colleague has been put on notice, she now inevitably feels some irritation of her own pursuant to the way that you conveyed your concerns. Granted, you do not have to deal with the anxiety and discomfort of viewing her reaction in the moment, nor do you have to worry about her pushing back and placing you on the hot seat to respond in the moment. Nonetheless, in some way and at some point, you will have to deal with her reactions to your e-mail. Whether she confronts you in person or via e-mail, or alternatively avoids a confrontation altogether and engages in passive-aggressive undermining, there will be an impact of some fashion from your communication.

This example emphasizes the importance of being mindful about how we communicate. Whether we are communicating in person or electronically, it is vital always to employ the healthy communication and conflict engagement strategies articulated in this chapter. The simplest and most effective way to stay on track during electronic communication is always to make a point of reviewing your words before you click the "send" button and asking yourself if you would dare to say the same in person. If the answer is no, there may very well be something about the way you have communicated that warrants modification and refinement. We live in an age when electronic communication is inevitable and, for purposes of practicality and convenience, we rely heavily on expressing ourselves through these indirect methods. This is fine as long as we do not use electronic communication to facilitate bravery and risk taking that we otherwise would be unable to assert.

Conflict is an inevitable part of academic life and, for most people, conflict is challenging. The challenge of effectively handling conflict is heightened for those in a less powerful position as a junior faculty member, and even more so for black junior faculty. By virtue of being people of color within a predominantly white institution, black junior faculty are in incredibly vulnerable positions, especially when conflicts arise. Whether or not the conflict itself is racially based, race shapes the nuances of how conflicts are expressed, perceived, responded to, and evaluated. As a black junior faculty member, you will repeatedly face the challenge of deciding when to engage in a conflict and how to do so in a way that will result in an effective resolution to the specifics of the issue at hand and the broader politics of race. In this chapter, we detailed how to distinguish healthy from unhealthy conflict, and provided directions and strategies for effectively engaging in and resolving conflicts. We discussed the dangers inherent in avoiding (and engaging in) conflict in general and for black academics, offering suggestions for distinguishing between times when it is best to push back and pull back from a conflict in light of multiple factors, especially the realities of race.

Suggested Readings

Hardy, Kenneth, and Tracey Laszloffy. (1995). "Therapy with African Americans and the Phenomenon of Rage." In *Sessions: Journal of Psychotherapy* 1, no. 4: 57–70.

Patterson, Kerry, Joseph Grenny, Ron McMillan, and Al Switzler. (2002). *Crucial Conversations: Rules for Talking When Stakes Are High.* New York: McGraw-Hill.

Rosenberg, Marshall. (2003). *Nonviolent Communication: A Language of Life.* Encinitas, CA: Puddledancer Press.

Stone, Douglas, Bruce Patton, Sheila Heen, and Roger Fisher. (2000). *Difficult Conversations: How to Discuss What Matters Most.* New York: Penguin Books.

Ursiny, Tim. (2003). *Coward's Guide to Conflict: Empowering Solutions for Those Who Would Rather Run Than Fight.* Naperville, IL: Sourcebooks.

Weeks, Dudley. (1994). *Eight Essential Steps to Conflict Resolution.* Los Angeles: Tarcher Press.

Weiner, David. (2002). *Power Freaks: Dealing with Them in the Workplace or Any Place.* New York: Prometheus.

10 | Building a Supportive Network

WE are relational beings and, as such, community is essential to our survival. Each of us varies in the extent to which we desire or require support from others, but all of us need community to some extent. During times when we are under stress and faced with adversity and hardships, community plays a particularly vital role in our capacity to endure. As we have detailed at length, the position of junior faculty in the academy is fraught with challenges that are demanding and stressful on many levels. These challenges are intensified and multiplied for black faculty. Consequently, we cannot overstate the role that community plays in helping black faculty to successfully navigate the rocky road to tenure.

Though all of the strategies we have presented thus far play an important part in achieving tenure without losing your soul, none of them can be effective in the absence of establishing and maintaining supportive relational networks. In fact, you may have already noticed that many of the concepts and strategies mentioned in the preceding chapters assume the importance of community. In this final chapter, however, we focus our attention on articulating specific strategies and actions that faculty can employ to purposefully, actively, and intentionally seek out, cultivate, and sustain relational networks that will provide essential support throughout their academic careers.

New Job, New City, No Support

One of the many challenges of academic life is that the job market is national as opposed to local. This often requires that new faculty start their

175

life on the tenure track in a new and unfamiliar city where they have no existing social, intellectual, or community support network. Because of the nature of the academic calendar, this life transition begins in the summer months that precede the first day of your faculty position. During that short period of time, you will move to your new location while simultaneously completing the requirements for graduation and preparing courses for the fall (that you may be teaching for the first time). In other words, building new relationships, seeking instrumental and psychosocial support, and meeting people in your new community are rarely at the top of a packed list of priorities. However, we argue that creating a broad network of support from the beginning of your career is one of the most important priorities for black faculty. In this chapter, we outline specific types of relationships that you will want to consider cultivating at the outset of your career to reduce alienation and increase productivity.

In order to create a truly comprehensive network of support, there are three pillars that black faculty should develop as early in their career as possible: (1) supportive social relationships on and off campus, (2) professional mentors, and (3) accountability partners. As we did in previous chapters, we encourage all faculty to proactively cultivate a broad network of support. Too many of us wait for others to reach out to us. By the time we figure out that is not going to happen, it is so late in our tenure clock that we have missed the benefit of a rich local and national network of mentors, friends, social service providers, and accountability partners. This is particularly critical for black faculty because they are at risk of developing a sense of alienation based on their underrepresentation (or solo status) among the faculty at their institution and because inevitable encounters with racial insensitivities and injustices are likely to exacerbate existing feelings of isolation and lack of support.

Supportive Relationships

During this discussion about what constitutes a supportive relationship, we encourage you to think about multiple areas of your life. We specifically address **on-campus support**, **off-campus support**, and **the national community** of your profession, but these are only three of numerous potential areas where you can build a network of support. As you read about the three areas that we focus on here, you may want to consider additional types of relational networks that are unique to your particular circumstances (e.g., community organizations, local schools, activist networks).

Creating On-Campus Support

Although institutions understand that new faculty require assistance in becoming acclimated to their new environment and professional support to move forward on the tenure track, most new faculty are unaware of all the support services that exist as part of the organizational structure of their college and university. There may be a **new faculty support program**, a **mentoring program**, a **professional development series**, or all of these. Each of these types of organizational programs provides built-in opportunities to make important social connections and eases the awkwardness of doing so by creating structured opportunities for networking. These programs vary by institution and, in our experience, can be as limited as a one-hour new faculty orientation or as fully developed as a five-week new faculty colloquium series that includes weekly dinner with the college dean. You may have to ask directly about what programs exist. If your department chair is not knowledgeable about the services that are available, you will have to be proactive in obtaining this information from another person or unit.

Creating Off-Campus Support Networks

Establishing a system of support off campus can be particularly challenging if your first faculty position is located in an unfamiliar city or town. Because of the large amount of time spent working while on the tenure track, new faculty sometimes forget the importance of building a well-rounded network of support. The first thing to determine is the types of relationships outside of your professional life that are most important to you. For Kerry Ann, it is important to have non-university friends, to have strong relationships with her neighbors and local community, to belong to a local church, to selectively participate in community organizations that work for social change, and to have a weekly appointment with a therapist. When she moved to Chicago, Kerry Ann was proactive in setting aside time each week during her first semester to find a church, attend neighborhood meetings, get a referral for a good local therapist who accepted her insurance, and select a local school in which to invest her volunteer time and energy. Each of these activities is important to Kerry Ann because it fulfills a different supportive need. Church meets her spiritual needs and also provides intergenerational and cross-class relationships. A weekly therapy appointment allows her to discuss relationships and emotional pressures before a crisis emerges. Relationships with neighbors fill her need for community and facilitate reciprocal assistance around home-based needs. Most important to Kerry Ann is having nonacademic friends in whom she can confide because this allows her to keep work relationships largely professional and to maintain healthy boundaries with colleagues.

The networks of support for other faculty may not look at all like Kerry Ann's because their relational needs and the places where they feel comfortable having those needs met may be completely different. Some of our colleagues fulfill their needs for community and intergenerational relationships by hanging out at a local bar, others stop by a barbershop or beauty salon weekly, and still others frequent their favorite gym. Faculty who relocate with a family may find they require fewer support mechanisms than those who are single. It is less important to follow a particular format and more important to determine your personal support needs, then proactively set up a support network to meet them.

The National Community

At the beginning of your career, it is important to learn about the professional organizations that exist beyond the main national organization for your discipline (which you presumably joined in graduate school). Every discipline has multiple organizations that cater to specific subgroups, and these can be great ways to further build your support network. In most disciplines, there is a specific organization for black academics or for those studying black issues from the discipline's perspective. Some examples are the Association of Black Sociologists, the National Black Nurses Association, the Association of Black Anthropologists, the National Conference of Black Social Workers, the National Institutes of Health Black Scientists Association, and the National Conference of Black Political Scientists. Alternatively, there may be a caucus or section in your discipline's national organization that serves a similar purpose.

One benefit of joining a variety of professional organizations that match your interests is that you can stay connected electronically to opportunities in your field through Listservs and discussion forums. Often, a specialty group is the filter for fellowships, postdocs, jobs, and publishing opportunities that are directly in your subarea, which can help to narrow down the overwhelming flow of information available.

Finally, you may want to consider joining various types of electronic communities. We created the discussion forum at Black Academic.com to provide an electronic meeting place where black faculty and graduate students could participate in a mentoring community. All a new faculty member has to do is log on to the forum, then ask any question (anonymously) or start a discussion on any professional development topic. Many faculty have found that the forum is a valuable way to find answers to questions they are too embarrassed to ask others, to test out their ideas about how to manage a conflict, or to vent about a difficult situation that has occurred in their department.

Building Your Brand

From the inception of your career, you must devote focused attention on building a national reputation for yourself (as a scholar) and your research. It is important for all junior faculty to do this as a way to form a compelling case for promotion and tenure, but it is especially important for black faculty. Developing a **national reputation** is a means of buffering yourself against some of the institutionalized racism that is likely to surface as you pursue promotion. A national reputation will strengthen your position, making yourself too valuable for an institution to lose. The more you become recognized "out there," the more weight you will carry in the university or college. It is one of the precious few means of buying yourself a piece of power and, given the forces working against you, you will need every source of strength that it is possible to accumulate.

Part of developing a national reputation involves the one activity that academics find horrifying: **self-promotion**. Although we acknowledge that self-promotion can be ugly, we also want to emphasize that your publications are currency in the academic market and are essential to the success of your professional career. Keep in mind that somewhere between four and eight senior faculty members from other institutions who are the top researchers in your subfield will be asked to serve as external reviewers of your **tenure packet**. Those external reviewers need to know who you are and to be somewhat familiar with your work before they receive your packet. As a result, it is important that you make a list of the top twenty scholars in your research area and set a goal of trying to meet four of them per year. Whether you encounter these researchers at annual meetings of your national professional association, contact them directly to request feedback on some of your work, or invite them to give a lecture at your institution, there are numerous ways to introduce yourself. These are the academics who will most value your scholarship and who will interact with you (and your work) during the greater part of your career—so get to know them!

As difficult as it may be to engage in, self-promotion is critical to your success. Every writer wants others to read his work and connect with the ideas. But the reality is that many brilliant articles and books are never read because of the sheer volume of work that is produced each year. Merely writing a smart paper will not set you apart from the pack. As one of Kerry Ann's advisers used to say: "Honey, get out there and shake it!" While sexist and horrifying in the moment uttered, it was a well-intentioned way of encouraging a new faculty member to proactively share her work. You can do this in several ways. For example, give lectures about your work at other institutions whenever invited. If you have not been invited anywhere, offer to chair your department's lecture series. Then, invite as lecturers people you *already know* (who will reciprocate by inviting you to their department for a talk), people whom you *want to know* (the "big names" in your subfield), people whom your department faculty *need to know* (especially if you are the only person in your department working in a particular subfield), and people who are *serving in important roles* (i.e., the editor of your flagship journal). Each time a lecturer comes to campus presents an opportunity to familiarize another scholar with your work. Ask in advance if she will meet with you during her visit and, if so, be sure to have copies of your work for her to take home.

Give lectures yourself to serve as "advertising" both before and after you publish a major article or book. Tell other scholars in your subfield about your publications, and ask your editor to send them complimentary copies of your article or book for adoption in their courses. Consider hiring a publicist for your first book to facilitate connections to media outlets in your subject area. Let your institution's Public Relations Office know who you are, what you do, and when your book is coming out. Finally, set up and maintain your own departmental website and register it with the major search engines. This will allow anyone who is looking for you, especially researchers doing work in your area, to find you.

Of course, one of the best opportunities for meeting other scholars in your field and promoting your work is professional conferences. Although it is important to attend the annual meetings of your national professional organization, you may find that small, subfield-specific conferences will provide the greatest bang for your buck. We encourage you to invest heavily in preparing presentations for conferences so that your paper will stand out for content as well as clarity. Given that unclear and poorly timed presentations are the norm, it is not difficult to give a presentation that stands out at most conferences. But in addition to presenting papers, you must learn how to "work it" at any conference you attend. That means contacting people in advance to set up meetings, being well groomed, having business cards ready and handy, developing a thirty-second shtick to describe what you do in a compelling way, and learning to maneuver at large receptions. All of these are learned skills that can make you someone who immediately comes to mind when other scholars think about your area of research.

Cultivating Mentors and Sponsors

We frequently hear about the importance of mentoring, yet it has become clear to us over time that mentoring is neither well understood nor clearly defined. We all know that mentoring is important to our success and mobility, but what exactly is mentoring? We hold a broad view of **mentoring** that includes the process of professional socialization and the sharing of information (not written or widely available) that is critical to success. Because there are multiple dimensions to your position, there are multiple dimensions in which you will require mentoring: teaching, research, service, and general professional development.

We also believe it is important to distinguish between mentors and sponsors in your professional life. While **mentors** pass on the unwritten rules of success in your area, **sponsors** are people who use their power on your behalf. For example, a senior faculty member may act as a mentor by having lunch with you, reading and critiquing your papers, and providing advice on what service requests to accept. That colleague may be incredibly helpful to you on a regular basis, and thus fits the definition of a mentor. Yet when behind closed doors with other faculty, the same person may choose not to say anything on your behalf when you are being discussed, not to mention your name when important opportunities arise, and not to speak highly of you when given the opportunity. These latter activities are the work done by sponsors and, in this colleague, you would have a wonderful mentor, but not a sponsor. It is also the case that you may have senior faculty in your life who act as sponsors but have no time whatsoever to mentor you. Both mentors and sponsors are critical to success, yet too often the crucial role that sponsors play in the professional advancement of junior faculty members is not so well understood.

Good mentors and sponsors are not easy to find. If your institution has a junior faculty mentoring program, that is a good starting place. However, we know of few black faculty who have found useful mentors through matching programs. You likely will need to be proactive in seeking out mentors. Sponsors are even more difficult to find, but seem to emerge as junior faculty show signs of success at their institution and in their disciplinary subfield. Below we list some proactive ways for you to find mentors, instead of waiting for mentors to find you:

- *Professional organizations.* Many professional organizations have mentor-matching programs that will provide you with a mentor if you request one.
- *Science, Technology, Engineering, and Mathematics (STEM) disciplines.* There is an organization called mentor.net that provides institutions with a service to match underrepresented graduate students and junior faculty with mentors in both academe and industry.
- *Word of mouth.* Let people know you are looking for a particular type of mentor. For example, "I am looking for a mentor who can relate to my experience of being a woman on the tenure track with two young children. If you know someone who fits that description, please let me know."
- *People in your department.* Approach faculty and tell them that you would like to receive mentoring in a specific area. For example, you might say, "I want to become a more effective facilitator of discussion in small seminars. I have heard you are great at that. I'm wondering if I could come to observe your class, and afterward maybe you and I could have coffee to discuss the techniques that you use and how they might be effective for me."

Creating Mechanisms for Accountability

One of the most difficult factors facing tenure-track faculty is the balance of research, teaching, and service. Too often, junior faculty feel pulled in several directions and end up unconsciously reacting first to the demands that have impending deadlines. In other words, we often prioritize things in our minds, not according to their importance in our quest for tenure but instead according to what we have to answer for in the immediate moment. The end result is that typical new faculty members spend a huge amount of time on teaching because class schedules are such that they have to stand in front of a group of students once, twice, or three times per week and teach. Classes thus act as small, ongoing deadlines that force us to move forward each week toward our pedagogical goals. They provide a regular, built-in **accountability mechanism** that, like it or not, we must answer to each week during the semester.

To a lesser extent, service commitments also have built-in accountability. Scheduled meetings, events, and bureaucratic deadlines provide firm dates and times that we must be present and prepared. The problem is that the most important activities on which tenure-track faculty will be evaluated for tenure and promotion have no built-in deadlines or accountability. Instead, we are left to our own internal discipline and strategic planning to map a research agenda, engage in research, and publish the findings. It is precarious to rely on the annual departmental reviews, third year review, and tenure review in the sixth year as our only accountability.

Some faculty do thrive on their own, but many spend the majority of their time teaching in the first three years only to panic at the third year review. This results in an anxiety-filled race to the finish line during the second half of their tenure-track experience. Our hope is that you will begin taking preventive measures today if you are already in that trap or think you could fall into it. The key is to create your own accountability mechanism that, like class each week, will force you to move forward.

Writing Accountability Groups

You will recall from Chapter 6 how the research of Robert Boice illustrated that the greatest writing gains were made by faculty members who not only wrote daily and recorded their progress, but were accountable to someone else on a weekly basis. There are several different models of creating accountability around writing and publication, including (1) traditional writing groups, (2) writing accountability groups, (3) write on-site gatherings, (4) online writing clubs, and (5) individual writing coaches. We explore each of these formats briefly to point out their structure, their strengths, and the types of faculty for whom they work best.

1. Traditional writing groups. In the traditional format of writing groups, a group of faculty members with similar substantive interests gets together once a month to read and comment on each other's written work. This involves preparing your own draft once per semester and reading one other faculty member's draft each month, writing comments, and gathering to discuss it at the monthly meeting. **Traditional**

writing groups require quite a lot of preparation and time (reading the draft, preparing comments, and meeting), and they offer varying degrees of useful feedback to the writer. If they are well organized, faculty receive high-quality feedback on their papers. But when they are poorly organized, drafts are returned with largely editorial comments that faculty could have received from a professional editor without the cost in time of reading the drafts of others. The strength of traditional writing groups is that they provide substantive feedback from colleagues in your field. The constraints are that the feedback can vary in quality, participation requires a significant time commitment, and the groups rarely provide social support, community building, or mentoring because they are organized solely around critiquing papers.

2. Writing accountability groups. Unlike traditional writing groups, faculty in **writing accountability groups** do not read each other's work, but instead meet once a week to ensure that there is a group present to witness the promises each member makes to himself or herself. In other words, accountability groups are designed to stimulate writing productivity by demystifying the writing and publication process, acknowledging the emotional and personal issues involved in writing, and providing a supportive communal environment where junior faculty can hold each other responsible for achieving their self-defined goals. Groups are ideally composed of four members (one tenured and three tenure-track faculty) from different colleges and departments. This ensures that participation is naturally expansive to everyone's network and that the participants are not tempted to start reading each other's work (and forget about accountability). During the one-hour group meeting, every faculty member gives a fifteen-minute oral report that restates his writing goal for the previous week, informs the group about whether or not he met the goal, describes what happened if he did not meet his goal, and states his goal for the following week. This formula allows each group member to learn how to set achievable weekly goals and to discuss the obstacles that prevented him from writing. Whenever problems arise, group members work to collectively strategize about how to solve them.

Writing accountability groups try to move faculty beyond simply engaging in daily writing to a place where they are producing completed drafts that can be circulated to editors, trusted assessors, and experts in the field. These groups are considered successful when all the members have developed a healthy, sustainable writing routine and have completed their semester work plan. Some groups bond and stay together for years, others change members each semester, and still others modify the basic format to accommodate the personality of the group. These groups present no significant costs in time, and require organization only at the beginning of the semester and a firm commitment for one hour a week from participants.

3. Write on-site gatherings. As an entirely different model of a writing group, some faculty get together once per week to literally write in a common space for a designated period of time. The groups can be large or small, and members make a commitment to attend weekly, arrive on time, and not disturb others. We both have participated in such **write on-site gatherings** and have been amazed by the positive energy and excitement that emerge when fifteen people descend on a coffee shop to write for two hours. This kind of gathering can be held on or off campus and requires only a core group to set a time and place. Often, the group stays for a meal or snack afterward to socialize and exchange information.

4. Online writing clubs. For faculty who are unable to organize a writing group, desire more frequent check-ins, or simply prefer an online alternative, there are **online writing clubs** that allow for daily accountability, support, and community. Online accountability groups operate on the same basic principles as accountability groups that meet in person. They are organized, however, around monthly "writing challenges" wherein faculty post their writing goals for the month, commit to a minimum of one hour per day of writing, and post their progress every day at the end of their writing time. Daily posts include a description of progress, any obstacles that arose, a treat or reward for completing the daily writing commitment, and a statement of goals for the following day. Similar to the accountability groups, a discussion of writing quickly opens the door for various professional development topics, mentoring, and group problem solving. The online groups are a particularly useful way for faculty who work in geographically isolated locations to experience support and mentoring from a national community of black academics, as opposed to being solely dependent on the faculty available in their particular campus. The strength of online writing groups is that they provide a high degree of accountability (via the daily check-in), require explicit goal setting, and provide a strong measure of social support (albeit virtual). The downsides are that some faculty experience difficulty in maintaining the daily commitments and, although some groups are free, most cost approximately $50.00 per month to join.

5. An individual writing coach. Faculty who require high levels of accountability and individualized attention in order to develop a healthy writing routine may want to consider hiring an **individual writing**

coach during their first semester or year on the tenure track. Typically, these faculty work with a writing coach (in person or via phone) once a week for a forty-five-minute session. During that time, the faculty member reports on weekly progress as well as the obstacles faced during the week. Time is spent in the coaching session on specific problem solving, time management, and working toward the completion of the faculty member's goals. The strength of coaching as an accountability mechanism is that it provides highly individualized attention. The constraint is the cost (on average $100 per session), which some faculty pay out of their professional development funds negotiated as part of their start-up package.

Summary

This chapter outlined how black faculty can build comprehensive support networks. We suggested that, early in their careers, black faculty need to cultivate at least three pillars: (1) supportive social relationships on and off campus, (2) professional mentors, and (3) accountability partners. Establishing strong and rich social networks is especially critical for black faculty because they are at risk of encountering racial insensitivities and injustices and consequently feeling marginalized, isolated, and alienated. Specific guidelines were also offered on how faculty can identify and nurture relationships with sponsors and mentors, and how they can establish accountability mechanisms that are vital components of supportive relational networks geared to foster optimal faculty success.

Suggested Readings

Antonio, Anthony. (2002). "Faculty of Color Reconsidered." *Journal of Higher Education* 73, no. 5: 582–602.
Benjamin, Lois. (Ed.). (1997). *Black Women in the Academy: Promises and Perils*. Gainesville: University Press of Florida.
Christensen, Carole Pigler. (1994). "Undue Duress: Minority Women in Academia." *Journal of Ethno-Development* 3: 77–85.
Cooper, Tuesday. (2006). *The Sista' Network: African-American Women Successfully Negotiating the Road to Tenure*. New York: Anker.
Cornelius, Llewellyn J., Sharon E. Moore, and Muriel Gray. (1997). "The ABCs of Tenure: What All African-American Faculty Should Know." *The Western Journal of Black Studies* 21, no. 3: 150–155.

Dixon-Reeves, Regina. (2003). "Mentoring as a Precursor to Incorporation: An Assessment of the Mentoring Experience of Recently Minted Ph.D.s." *Journal of Black Studies* 34: 12–27.

Edmondson, Belinda. (1995). "The Double Bind of Black Women in the Academy." *The Monthly Forum on Women in Higher Education.*

Fenelon, James. (2003). "Race, Research, and Tenure: Institutional Credibility and the Incorporation of African, Latino, and American Indian Faculty." *Journal of Black Studies* 34: 87–100.

Fields, Cheryl D. (1996). "A Morale Dilemma: Black Professors on White Campuses." *Black Issues in Higher Education.*

Moses, Yolanda T. (1989). *Black Women in Academe: Issues and Strategies.* Washington, DC: Association of American Colleges.

Phillip, Mary-Christine. (1994). "Breaking the Silence: Black Women Academics Meet." *Black Issues in Higher Education* 10, no. 25: 14.

Tillman, Linda. (2001). "Mentoring African American Faculty in Predominantly White Institutions." *Research in Higher Education* 42, no. 3: 295–325.

Turner, Caroline. (2003). "Incorporation and Marginalization in the Academy." *Journal of Black Studies* 34: 112–125.

Weems, Robert. (2003). "The Incorporation of Black Faculty at Predominantly White Institutions: A Historical and Contemporary Perspective." *Journal of Black Studies* 34: 101–111.

PART 4
Conclusion

11 | Succeeding with Integrity

IN the preceding pages, we have addressed how to succeed as a junior faculty member in terms of teaching well and effectively, publishing prolifically, and performing meaningful service. Although many of the technical strategies detailed for building a strong tenure case are general and can be used by any junior faculty, irrespective of race, there are numerous ways in which the application of and response to these strategies are colored by the subtleties of race and racism. We have gone to great lengths to identify when and where race and racism shape the ways in which black academics pursue excellence in terms of their teaching, scholarship, and service. And in every way imaginable, we have tried to be explicit about how black faculty can effectively negotiate the dilemmas imposed by racism while still retaining their integrity and soul. Far too often, the combination of being in a vulnerable position as both a junior faculty member and a racial minority has led many black faculty to sacrifice everything—their relationships, their voice, their integrity—in the pursuit of tenure and promotion. As we have discussed throughout the book, there is no victory in winning tenure if you sacrifice your core self in the process. Worse yet is to end up losing your soul and *still* not winning tenure. This is why we have devoted so much attention to addressing the conditions and dynamics that factor into maintaining integrity and dignity as you pursue tenure.

To be a black academic in the United States today is to live a life that was only a dream but a few generations ago. For hundreds of years, black people were denied the opportunity to learn to read and write; therefore, in the struggle for freedom, we have always understood that education is a pathway for liberation. Accordingly, the presence of black faculty in the halls of academe is a sweet victory. It speaks to the remarkable strides that have been gained by the many people who struggled against adversity for social transformation. Moreover, to be a black faculty member is to be the beneficiary of a quality education, and it implies an opportunity to directly extend this legacy to others.

For all the strides that have been gained, however, a book like this one is necessary because the story of race in the United States continues to be a story steeped in inequality and injustice. Current events plainly highlight that, as much as things have improved, white supremacy continues to shape a US landscape in which race and racism persist. As much as many of us wish to live in a truly color-blind society (devoid of racial inequalities and racism), we continue to exist in a racially divided, white supremacist society. And it is within this context that black junior faculty must work to win tenure while struggling not to lose their soul in the process.

To be black in the United States means to struggle. Whatever particular circumstances define a black person's life, the realities of race are such that most are confronted by barriers and blocks. As a black academic, you are not exempt from this fundamental truth. And yet, despite the challenges, you must succeed. Like those who came before you fighting so hard against the odds to survive and be successful, you too must find the inner fortitude to persevere in spite of the challenges. Each of us has the power of *personal agency*, which means that, whatever pitfalls are placed in our pathway, we can choose how we will manage adversity.

As we discussed in earlier portions of the book, the nature of oppression is that the oppressed are caught in a *double bind*, meaning that, to some extent, whatever choice is exercised, they are likely to lose something essential. In the context of this book, we detailed an essential dilemma facing black academics: "choosing" not to confront racism as an attempt to enhance the chances of securing tenure at the risk of losing the soul versus "choosing" to push back against racial insensitivities and assaults to retain dignity at the risk of undermining tenurability. It is a catch-22. There is no perfect choice. Every choice is likely to involve some kind of loss. And yet, we want to go on record as advocating for the importance of siding with your soul.

We wrote this book because we believe in the value of simultaneously making a flawless tenure case according to the stated rules of the game while never surrendering your soul in the process. We realize that the work of maintaining dignity means you run the risk of being labeled as a troublemaker or someone who is difficult or even angry, and labels like these can work against tenure. But at the end of the day, we trust in the worth of being the best you can academically while also remaining faithful to your integrity. In doing this, whatever outcome you face with regard to tenure, you will ultimately win. If you win tenure, it will be with the satisfaction that comes from knowing you did not compromise yourself for this victory. If you do not win tenure, you will have the satisfaction that comes from knowing this decision was not a reflection of your capability, skill, or effort and that what was lost in terms of justice and the benefits of tenure was gained with respect to your dignity. And because you are a talented and gifted person, you can walk away to seek another opportunity and continue your journey, pressing forward like the ancestors whose sacrifices made it possible for you to take on this fight in the first place.

Some of the greatest assets you will have in your journey toward tenure and beyond are the ties you forge and nurture with others. Black people have survived centuries of trauma through the power of community, and today this remains a priceless resource. As alone as you may sometimes feel, there are others who struggle similarly, and the key to survival lies in collective struggle.

A parting thought we wish to convey above all else is that we hope you will use the power bestowed on you by the victory of being granted tenure to challenge and transform the system. Of course, many believe that, once they "make it," they will actually use their powers "for good." And yet history is filled with the all-too-true tales of those who, upon making it, quickly forget the struggle to get there. As clichéd as it sounds, power corrupts. The comforts that come with achievements like tenure can seduce the best of us to melt into the rhythms of the status quo instead of using this newfound power as leverage in the fight to radically remake the system that has now granted us benefits.

The temptation to collude with the status quo is heightened by the fear that, even with the power that comes with tenure, you are not safe. It is striking how many black academics have reported to us that they still feel vulnerable and at risk after having been granted tenure. Even the protections provided by tenure are not always enough to protect against the inherent injustices of racism. And if we are never really safe, it begs the question: at one point do we dare to press for change?

There are no simple answers to these questions. Most likely, you are reading this book because you are a junior faculty member, or poised to become one, at an institution. This is a victory in and of itself that was made possible by the sacrifices of those who came before you. You are at this point today because many were brave when it was not safe and were willing to risk much with few rewards for themselves personally.

In so doing, they helped to make your dreams possible. So whatever adversities you have faced and will continue to face, remember those who came before. Stay true to their spirit and the sheer willpower they manifested in refusing to be humbled into staying silent when it may have seemed "easier" or more expedient to do so. There will be pressures on you to bow down as you encounter racial insensitivities and assaults both before and after winning tenure. You may be tempted to just go along instead of pushing back, rationalizing your collusion with the system as a much-earned reprieve from the constant necessity to fight or because of fear that you remain at risk even with tenure. But whatever may be your internal conflicts and challenges, we ask you to *never forget*. Never forget the shoulders that supported you in the journey to where you are today. Never forget the sacrifices that paved the way for your opportunities. And never forget the corresponding responsibility you bear to do your part to make choices that will extend these opportunities to those who follow you.

Index

Academic diversity officers, 36
Academic freedom, 11, 53
Academic job market: competition in, 52; national nature of, 175; research publications as currency in, 63
Academic office, 7; chaos in, 69; filing systems in, 83–88; functional efficiency and, 75; impression management and, 70–73, 74, 87; institutional norms and, 73–75, 88; people encouraged to linger at, 71–73; productivity influenced by, 69; questions about, 69; tips for, 87–88. *See also* Organization, of office
Academic perfectionism, 97–99
Academic socialization, 43–44
Academic system: change resisted by, 32; common experiences of racism in, 12; hierarchical nature of, 11; race, power, and, 11–29
Acceptable conduct, 21
Accountability mechanisms, 7; creating, 182–186; group, 65, 183–186; teaching and, 108
Action box, 83
Addictions, 126–127, 128
Administrative jobs, 103
Affirmative action hire, 110
Alcohol, 127, 128
Alienation, 3, 13, 14–17, 130, 136, 176

Allies, lacking, 155
Alternative behaviors, 147–148
Anger, 133, 136, 137, 144, 167–168
Annual review, 20, 151, 155–158, 166–167
Appointments, 64
Art of efficient teaching and service, 7; balance program for, 112–117; saying no and, 118–120; tips for, 120; typical new faculty members and, 107–111
Authoritative style, of leadership, 39
The Autobiographies of Malcolm X, 138
Avoidance, 142
Awards, 20

Balance program, for black faculty: difficulty of following, 117; discuss research and teaching with colleagues step of, 116; integrate research into teaching step of, 115–116; keep daily records of work time expenditure step of, 116–117; limit classroom preparation step of, 112–114; write daily step of, 114–115
Battle fatigue, 23
Belonging, diplomacy negotiated with, 16–17
Black faculty: all black people represented by, 15–16; assumptions of diversity work responsibilities

About the Book

FOR an African American scholar, who may be the lone minority in a department, navigating the tenure minefield can be a particularly harrowing process. Kerry Ann Rockquemore and Tracey Laszloffy go beyond standard professional resources to serve up practical advice for black faculty intent on playing, and winning, the tenure game.

Addressing head-on how power and the thorny politics of race converge in the academy, *The Black Academic's Guide* is full of invaluable tips and hard-earned wisdom. It is an essential handbook that will help black faculty survive and thrive in academia without losing their voices or their integrity.

Kerry Ann Rockquemore is associate professor of sociology and African American studies and founder of the Under-Represented Faculty Mentoring Program at the University of Illinois at Chicago. **Tracey Laszloffy** is a coach and therapist for black and Latino faculty at predominately white institutions. The two are cofounders of www.Black Academic.com, a website for minority scholars.